THE SUBJECT'S POINT OF VIEW

2008

The Subject's Point of View

Katalin Farkas

OXFORD
UNIVERSITY PRESS

This book has been printed digitally and produced in a standard specification in order to ensure its continuing availability

OXFORD
UNIVERSITY PRESS

Great Clarendon Street, Oxford OX2 6DP

Oxford University Press is a department of the University of Oxford.
It furthers the University's objective of excellence in research, scholarship,
and education by publishing worldwide in

Oxford New York

Auckland Cape Town Dar es Salaam Hong Kong Karachi
Kuala Lumpur Madrid Melbourne Mexico City Nairobi
New Delhi Shanghai Taipei Toronto

With offices in

Argentina Austria Brazil Chile Czech Republic France Greece
Guatemala Hungary Italy Japan South Korea Poland Portugal
Singapore Switzerland Thailand Turkey Ukraine Vietnam

Published in the United States
by Oxford University Press Inc., New York

Reprinted 2010

ISBN 978-0-19-923032-7

To my father, János László Farkas.

Preface

Externalism about the mind has been an intensively discussed and widely influential view for several decades. I think it is fair to say that internalist theories of mind are in the minority, and even those philosophers who defend some version of internalism often acknowledge that certain aspects of the mind need an externalist treatment. This book is part of a defence of an uncompromisingly internalist conception of the mind: that is, the view that all mental features are determined by the subject's internal states. Externalism, the view that some mental features constitutively depend on facts outside the subject, is mistaken.

The book has two parts, and the two parts can be read independently and in an optional order. Part Two relates more directly to some contemporary discussions about externalism, whereas Part One complements Part Two by offering the general motivations for internalism. Let me start now with describing what is in the second part.

In Chapter 4, which is the first chapter of Part Two, I address the question of how to define the controversy between internalism and externalism. According to the usual understanding, the issue depends on whether mental features are determined by facts inside or outside the subject's body or brain, but I argue that this understanding is unsatisfactory. Instead, internalism should be formulated as the view that the way things seem to a subject—the way things are from the subject's point of view—determine all her mental features. Externalism is the denial of this claim.

In Chapter 5, I defend the thesis that things seem the same for subjects if they share their internal phenomenal properties. Internalism is the view that the way things seem to me determines all my mental properties. In contrast, externalists say that things could seem exactly the same as they do now, and yet my mental properties could be different. In Chapter 6, I argue that, as a consequence, externalism limits the scope of privileged self-knowledge. I have privileged access only to how things seem to me. This must mean that, in the externalist view, there are mental properties that are not accessible in a privileged way, because their presence or absence cannot be registered among the facts that are accessible in a privileged way.

Considerations similar to those presented in Chapter 6—about self-knowledge, or autonomous action, or rationality—inclined a number of philosophers to sympathize with internalism, but it has been a constant worry that an internalist view of content cannot account for reference and truth. In Chapter 7, I try to show that this worry is unfounded.

Whereas Part Two relates to various debates in contemporary philosophy surrounding the internalism/externalism controversy, Part One is intended to offer a 'big picture'. In Chapter 1, I argue that privileged accessibility is the mark of the mental. That is, we classify our features into mental and non-mental features on the basis of the following criterion: what belongs to my mind is what is known to me in a way it is known to no one else. In Chapter 2, I answer some objections to this view. In Chapter 3, I claim that the significance of classifying features into mental and non-mental ones is to be found in the fact that we regard someone as a person, or as one of us, if they have the kind of mind we have. Since externalism posits mental features that lie outside the scope of privileged access—as I try to show in the second part—externalism comes into conflict with our fundamental conception of the mind.

I have worked on issues related to this book for many years, and have accumulated more intellectual debt than I can remember; I apologize to those whom I inadvertently miss out from the following list. I would like to thank Ferenc Altrichter and János Kelemen for vital encouragement at an early stage of my career. Ferenc Huoranszki and Howard Robinson have given me continuous support and discussed philosophy with me for many years, and I could not be where I am without their help. I am exceptionally fortunate to have been employed by the Central European University since 2000, and I am very grateful to the institution, as well as to my colleagues, Hanoch Ben-Yami, Gábor Betegh, István Bodnár, Mike Griffin, Ferenc Huoranszki, János Kis, Nenad Miščević, Howard Robinson, and David Weberman for providing a wonderful intellectual and collegial environment. I would like to acknowledge the support of the Hungarian OTKA, grant number 46757, and the Philosophy of Language Research Group of the Hungarian Academy of Sciences. I am also greatly indebted to the following people for discussions, comments, and advice: Gergely Ambrus, Kati Balog, Paul Boghossian, Manuel Liz, Barry Loewer, Mike Martin, Peter Momtchiloff, Gary Ostertag, Barry C. Smith, Zoltán Gendler Szabó, János Tőzsér, Tim Williamson, and Zsófia Zvolenszky. Two anonymous referees for Oxford University Press read a complete draft, and gave incredibly helpful and detailed comments, which resulted in significant changes, and hopefully improvements, in the book. I have discussed all these ideas (and all other ideas) with Tim Crane, and his influence is there on every page of this book, as well as in every day of my life.

And finally—I cannot remember exactly when or how I decided that I would become a philosopher, but I am sure that the fact that my father is a philosopher had something to do with it. To me, he will always remain the example of what it is to have genuine learning, uncompromising argumentative rigour, and endless intellectual curiosity. I dedicate this book to him with love and admiration.

K. F.

Contents

Analytical Table of Contents

Part One. Our Cartesian Mind

1 Privileged Access and the Mark of the Mental

1.1 The List

Richard Rorty claimed that many of our intuitions about the mind simply result from our uncritical reliance on the modern philosophical tradition originating from Descartes, but have no further significance. Rorty is right that our conception of the mind is essentially shaped by the Cartesian theory, but this book, unlike Rorty, suggests embracing, rather than overthrowing, this tradition.

1.2 The Project of the Second Meditation

Descartes's Second Meditation bears the title 'The nature of the human mind, and how it is better known than the body'. Descartes here considers the Aristotelian list of psychological faculties: nutritive, locomotive, sensory, and thinking capacities, and claims that only the last is essential to him.

1.3 Varieties of Thought

After he has established that he is a thinking thing, Descartes turns to the question of what a thinking thing is. His new understanding of 'sensory perceptions' makes it possible to include them as a form of 'thought'; applying Descartes's method, sensations, and emotions also turn out to be varieties of thought—that is, varieties of mental phenomena.

1.4 Incorporeal Minds and Certainty

How do we decide whether we regard a feature as belonging to the mind? Two suggestions are considered and rejected: that mental features are those that can be exemplified in an immaterial substance; and that mental features are those we cannot doubt we possess.

1.5 Special Access

Different cognitive faculties are distinguished. Only one of them has the following feature: it enables the subject to know its subject matter in a way that no one else who is endowed with the same cognitive faculty can. Everything that is known through the use of this faculty belongs to the mind. Privileged accessibility is the mark of the mental.

1.6 Cognitive Faculties

The cognitive faculty that provides special access to its subject matter is introspection. Introspection is distinguished from a priori knowledge—the kind of knowledge we have, for example, of logic and mathematics. Introspective justification is also distinguished from justification that is based on the contextually self-verifying nature of certain thoughts.

1.7 The Subject's Point of View

An explanation of why a portion of reality should be known to one person in a special way is advanced. Mental facts are perspectival facts; mental facts are characterized by how things are *for* the subject. To be a subject is to possess a point of view. This endows the subject with a prima facie authority, but does not provide her with infallibility in this area.

2 Unconscious, Conscious, Bodily

2.1 Access to the Body

One objection to the thesis that my mind is precisely what is known to me in a way that is known to no one else is that the same is true of certain states of my body. But this is contingent:

someone else could be appropriately 'wired' to my body and learn about its states, but she would not thereby learn about my *feelings* concerning these states.

2.2 Stream of Consciousness and Standing States

We distinguish between two types of mental phenomena: occurrent events, which are conscious and have a phenomenal character; and standing states, which are either not always conscious, or, according to some, never conscious. This latter position is also compatible with the main thesis of the book: when I know that, for example, I have a certain belief, I am conscious of *having* the belief, even if the belief itself is not conscious.

2.3 The Mind as an Ideal

Some clear counter-examples to the thesis that the mind is known to the subject in a privileged way are cases of repressed unconscious desires, or cases of self-deception. An argument given by Freud for the existence of the unconscious can be used to defend the Cartesian conception: our understanding of the unconscious is parasitic on our understanding of mental states that are available to conscious reflection.

3 Persons and Minds

3.1 The Importance of the Cartesian List

Our list of what belongs to the mind is the same as the Cartesian list of mental features, and rather different from, say, the Aristotelian list of psychological powers. Discarding the Cartesian conception may, therefore, be more difficult than some critics suggest, because it would require a fundamental change in our conception of the mental.

3.2 Citizen of Two Worlds

The present proposal is not committed to dualism about mind and body, but it does imply a certain duality about our nature: human beings are 'citizens of two worlds'. There is something in our nature that we share with the rest of the created world, and there is something that is distinctive of our mode of existence. The latter aspect is described here by saying that we are *persons*.

3.3 Questions about Persons

Four questions about persons are distinguished. First, do persons deserve a special treatment by other persons, and, if they do, what should this treatment be? Second, what sort of characteristics qualify a creature to be regarded as a person? Third, what is the ontological category to which persons belong? Fourth, what are the conditions for someone to remain the same person through time? Our interest here is in the second question.

3.4 Criteria of Personhood

The suggestion is that a person is a creature who has the kind of mind we have. Here lies the significance of the Cartesian conception of the mind: it offers us a list of mental phenomena that is put together on a principled basis; and it is the possession of more or less this list of mental attributes that provides the criteria for someone to be regarded as a person.

3.5 The Person and the Human Animal

It is explained why the suggestion of the previous section is compatible with various theories of personhood and personal identity; for example, with a Lockean theory or with an animalist theory.

3.6 Conclusion of Part One

Descartes's theory of the mind has received severe criticism in the twentieth and twenty-first centuries. This first part of this book has attempted to restore somewhat the reputation of the

Cartesian conception, even though the conception defended here departs from Descartes in a number of ways. The plan for Part Two is to argue that the characteristic feature of this conception is that it is internalist: it is committed to the claim that a subject's mental features are entirely determined by her internal properties.

Part Two. Internalism and Externalism

4 The Internal and the External

4.1 The Boundary Between the Internal and the External

The Twin Earth argument is briefly introduced. The conclusion of this argument is supposed to be that the content of our mental states is determined by facts external to us. The definition is incomplete unless we specify what 'internal' and 'external' mean.

4.2 Identity in Physical Make-Up

The usual set-up of the Twin Earth thought experiments relate the Twins by internal physical sameness. This is not sufficient to run a general externalist argument, for it fails to address dualist theories. It is not necessary for the externalist argument either, for externalism can arise with respect to facts inside the body.

4.3 External/Internal Defined

We attempt to define the external/internal relation by focusing on the relation between the Twins in the Twin Earth scenario: whatever is shared by the Twins is internal, and what is different is external. It is suggested that the relation between the Twins is the subjective indistinguishability of their situation—everything seems the same to them.

4.4 Twin Situations

A more precise understanding of 'subjective indistinguishability' is sought by listing situations that stand in this relation: a subject actually tasting water and counterfactually tasting a superficially similar liquid; an embodied subject and her brain-in-a-vat counterpart.

4.5 Physical or Functional Equivalence

The relation between the Twins cannot be defined as physical, functional, or merely behavioural equivalence. Instead, it should be defined in terms of sameness of some mental features (called here the 'metaphysical account') or in epistemic terms.

4.6 Phenomenal Properties Introduced

A sensory experience is an event of its appearing to a subject that things are in a certain way. In so far as two experiences involve things appearing in the same way, they share a phenomenal property. Phenomenal properties determine what it is like to have an experience. This notion of phenomenal properties can be extended to all conscious mental states, including cognitive states. The relation between the Twins is sameness of phenomenal properties of all their conscious mental life.

4.7 Narrow Content

It may be suggested that the relation between the Twins is sameness of narrow content of their mental states. This is accommodated by the previous proposal in so far as the phenomenally constituted intentional features are shared between the Twins.

4.8 Possible Objections to Phenomenal Properties

The suggestion that the relation constitutive of Twin situations is sameness of phenomenal properties faces some objections: that sameness of phenomenal properties is based on the 'same appearance relation', which is not transitive; and that, in

privileged way. This is somewhat obscured by the usual understanding of externalism, which draws the boundary between the internal and the external around the brain or the body.

6.2 **Internalism and Privileged Access**

All and only phenomenal properties of conscious events give rise to perspectival facts, which are precisely the facts that are open to privileged access. Phenomenal properties are shared by subjects in Twin situations. According to externalists, mental features are determined by factors that go beyond phenomenal properties, and hence they do not register within the subject's point of view. Compared to internalism, externalism limits privileged accessibility.

6.3 **Contextually Self-verifying thoughts**

Some externalists suggested an account of privileged self-knowledge that is perfectly compatible with externalism: that some reflective thoughts are justified because of their contextually self-verifying nature, and the consequent impossibility of their being false. This is not an adequate account of self-knowledge, because guaranteed correctness is compatible with ignorance, and because the account applies only to a small part of our conscious mental life.

6.4 **Externalism About Various Mental Features**

Externalism about content is the most frequently discussed form of externalism, but it is possible to be externalist about attitudes, or phenomenal character, or sensory features as well.

6.5 **Failure of Privileged Access**

Self-attributions of mental features other than content are not contextually self-verifying, and, if externalism about these features is accepted, these statements can easily be false. Here the limitation that externalism poses on privileged self-knowledge is obvious. In the cases of attributions of content, the limitation is obscured by the contextually self-verifying nature of the attribution.

6.6 Travelling Cases

My argument may resemble the structure of a popular argument for the incompatibility of externalism and self-knowledge: according to this argument, some form of discriminability is a necessary condition for knowledge, but subjects cannot discriminate their externally individuated thoughts. The debates surrounding this issue are partly due to the lack of clarity about which sense of 'discriminability' is in play in the argument.

6.7 Discrimination and Introspective Knowledge

When the claim that discrimination is necessary for knowledge is used in an argument, the reference is often to the work of Alvin Goldman, who defends the view that discrimination is necessary for perceptual knowledge. The notion Goldman uses is response discrimination; but, as was shown earlier, if content externalism is true, then Twin thoughts are response discriminable. Hence this argument for incompatibility does not work.

6.8 Access Discriminability and Introspective Knowledge

If the general necessary condition for knowledge is formulated in terms of access, rather than response discriminability, the result is still the same: if externalism is true, Twin situations are access discriminable. Hence the arguments for incompatibility that try to show a deficiency in the externalist's self-knowledge because of the failure of some general necessary discrimination condition do not work. My argument does not have this structure.

6.9 Discrimination Through Externally Individuated Contents

If discriminability—in both the response and the access sense—is due merely to externally individuated cognitive

7.2 The 'Inexpressibility of Narrow Content'

Contents are objects of mental attitudes. Defenders of dual-content—or dual-intentionality—theories occasionally claim that narrow contents are not expressible by using our language. This, if not fatal, is, in any case, an uncomfortable consequence for an internalist theory, and should be avoided, if possible.

7.3 Frege on Sense and Reference

The doctrine that sense determines reference is an expression of the idea that sense is responsible for semantic properties (truth and reference). Frege held the doctrine both for names and for sentences; in the latter case, he held that the sense of a sentence, a thought, determines a unique truth value. It seems that Frege actually believed that sense alone determines reference.

7.4 Aristotle on Beliefs and Truth Values

If a thought determines a truth value, then sentences with different truth values express different thoughts. Many people seem to accept this. But, for example, Aristotle, in the *Categories*, puts forward a different view: he thinks the truth value of a belief and statement can change, not because the belief is changing, but because of a change in the world. In that case, difference in truth value does not imply difference in content.

7.5 Same Content—Different Truth Value

The claim that sense alone determines reference (thought/content alone determines a truth value) may be plausible in the case of mathematics and logic. But an ordinary contingent descriptive sentence like 'the inventor of bifocals was a man' can be true in one world and false in another, while having the same content. This means that sense alone does not determine reference; that difference in truth value does not, in itself, imply difference in content.

7.6 Cross-World and Within-a-World Comparison

Many would perhaps accept that sense alone does not determine reference when we compare different possible worlds; but they may say that, within a world, difference in truth value or reference implies difference in sense. But this is merely a prejudice. If we have independent reasons to support this move, we can treat the within-the-world case analogously to the cross-world case.

7.7 Non-Indexical Contextualism

Contents need not be conceived as propositions whose truth value is fixed within a world. The present suggestion is similar to the view that John MacFarlane calls 'non-indexical contextualism', which treats context-sensitive expressions as expressing the same contents in different contexts, but receiving different references or truth values, because some change in a feature of the context is treated as a change in the circumstances of evaluation.

7.8 Double Indexing

Different features of a context may have different logical or semantic roles when determining semantic values; this is allowed by the present proposal. The important point is that their metaphysical status is the same: they are all external to the content. Distinguishing their semantic roles answers a certain objection by Kaplan.

7.9 Relativized Propositions

An objection by John Perry to a view similar to the present proposal is considered and answered.

7.10 The Inconclusiveness of the Twin Earth Argument

The classic Twin Earth argument in Putnam's formulation states that internalism is incompatible with the doctrine that sense determines reference. The foregoing shows that this is not correct. Since no one would want to claim that sense alone determines reference, if sense plus something else determines reference, the doctrine is still upheld. And this is precisely the idea behind my internalist theory.

7.11 Internalism with Truth Conditionality

This concludes the project of this book. The mind is essentially revealed from the subject's point of view. This conception lies at the heart of contemporary internalist theories. Moreover, internalism can account for truth conditionality; hence, overall, it is to be preferred to externalism.

PART ONE
Our Cartesian Mind

1

PRIVILEGED ACCESS AND THE MARK OF THE MENTAL

1.1 The List

What are we saying when we say that a creature has a mind? The answer may simply be that a creature has a mind if her history involves familiar mental features. Then one natural way to begin our enquiry about the mind would involve making a list of mental features. This list will include, say, thoughts, feelings, volitions, sense perceptions, emotions, beliefs, desires, pain, intentions, memory, and so on. The next step could be an attempt somehow to classify items on this list: to assort them into the categories of events, states, or properties; or, more specifically, propositional attitudes, phenomenal states, actions, and so on. Mapping out the territory in this way is not without complications; while trying to give an initial character of mental features and the categories they fall into, we are well on the way towards some fundamental problems in the philosophy of mind. For example, it may be tempting to draw up the list of the mental by contrasting it with the physical, and this could be the first step towards the emergence of the mind–body problem. Or we may wonder whether propositional attitudes and phenomenal states form mutually exclusive categories, and this question may further lead to the debate about the existence of qualia. And so on.

Intuitions about what we should put on the list of mental features show a remarkable convergence, at least in philosophical books (see, for example, the list of mental phenomena in standard reference books or textbooks such as Guttenplan 1994: 6, 24, Kim 1996: 13 ff, or Heil 1998). Every enquiry must start somewhere, and there is nothing wrong with such a procedure in itself. It seems, however, that we might hope to gain a deeper understanding of the issues involved if we tried to trace the origin of our list of mental features and the ensuing conception of the mind. This is especially true if doubts are raised about the propriety of considering this list as a starting point for our investigation. Richard Rorty (1980) begins his book *Philosophy and the Mirror of Nature* by reflecting on the phenomenon I have described above: that discussions in the philosophy of mind usually assume an intuitive compartmentalization of the world into the mental and the physical. He thinks this is a hangover from Cartesian dualism, preserved in the technical vocabulary of philosophers who grew up on texts of modern philosophy, but useless in illuminating any important issue in, or outside philosophy. The following paragraph sums it up well.

> I would hope ... to have incited the suspicion that our so-called intuition about what is mental may be merely our readiness to fall in with a specifically philosophical language-game. This is, in fact, the view that I want to defend. I think that this so-called intuition is no more than the ability to command a certain technical vocabulary—one which has no use outside of philosophy books and which links up with no issues in daily life, empirical science, morals or religion. (Richard Rorty 1980: 22)

Rorty is only one of the many twenty- and twenty-first-century critics of the Cartesian view of the mind, and other critics would possibly disagree with some of Rorty's own claims, which motivate his objections against the Cartesian tradition. I mention him in particular because his objection here concerns a very fundamental aspect of this tradition—the very notion of the mental. Answering him will, I hope, show what is in fact fundamentally right about this tradition.

In his book, as elsewhere, Rorty charges analytic philosophy with a lack of historical awareness: analytic philosophers pretend that problems and answers exist in their own right, outside a particular historical context. In contrast, true philosophical sensitivity requires that we identify the impact of the tradition that underlies our seemingly intuitive assumptions. But curiously, for Rorty—and for many similar self-professed 'historicists'—the main point of this enterprise is largely negative: we should discern historical influence in order to be able to overthrow it. Tradition—be it modern philosophy or even the whole course of Western philosophy—almost always has a negative effect according to this way of thinking: it burdens the discussion with unfounded presuppositions, baseless prejudices, misleading metaphors; it neglects the question of being, and so on. Once the historical influence on the formulation of a problem is shown, its contingent nature is revealed, thereby offering us encouragement to get rid of it. In favour of what, we might ask: are we finally in the position to correct the mistakes of the past, so that philosophical problems, once the sediment of tradition is scraped off, can shine in their true light? Hardly a historicist view. Or are we simply giving up one contingent influence in favour of another? If so, what is there to choose between them?

With a somewhat more positive attitude towards our philosophical predecessors, situating a problem in a historical context could serve another purpose: realizing to what extent our assumptions are shaped by certain historically developed views, we can get a deeper appreciation of how much we are bound by a certain way of thinking. The tradition then need not be overthrown; it can be embraced. In fact, this is what I hope to achieve in this book for an important aspect of our Cartesian legacy. The conception of the mental we have inherited from Descartes may not be as easy to discard as some critics have suggested; and, instead of being part of an esoteric conception confined to the realm of abstract philosophy, it is, I believe, fundamental to our understanding of ourselves as the kind of creatures we are.

Tracing the origins of a tradition may well promise another benefit. For, whenever the tradition started, someone must have had some reasons, other than simply following the tradition, to adopt certain questions and solutions, and we may hope to be able to address those reasons in their own right. If our list of mental features indeed originates with Descartes, at least we know where to look for the reasons. This is what I intend to do now. My aim is not a strict scholarly exercise in the interpretation of historical texts—in fact, as we shall see, I take certain liberties with some of Descartes's ideas. The reason for me to enlist his help is to try to address issues that are very much in the focus of contemporary philosophy of mind. I take Rorty's point that contemporary philosophers sometimes write as if they were in a historical vacuum, though perhaps this has happened less and less since 1980—possibly also because of Rorty's influence. As for me, invoking the historical context really helps me to make my case: for I want to highlight our Cartesian commitments by contrasting them with other possible influences in our philosophical tradition.

In this chapter, I shall attempt to capture the conception of mind that emerges from Descartes's *Meditations*. In the Second Meditation, Descartes systematically constructs a list of mental features that is different from the list of psychological features that he inherited from the previous philosophical tradition. I shall try to see what would be the most plausible method to put together such a list, and argue that it has to do with our different cognitive faculties and their subject matters.

1.2 The Project of the Second Meditation

Descartes's Second Meditation bears the title 'The nature of the human mind, and how it is better known than the body'.[1] We join

[1] References to Descartes's works are to *The Philosophical Writings of Descartes*, vols. i and ii, ed. and trans. John Cottingham, Robert Stoothoff, and Dugald Murdoch (Cambridge: Cambridge University Press, 1984–5) (CSM), and vol. iii (a selection of Descartes's letters), ed. and trans. John Cottingham, Robert Stoothoff, Dugald Murdoch, and Anthony Kenny (Cambridge: Cambridge University Press, 1991) (CSMK). As customary, I shall also give references to *Œuvres de Descartes*, ed. Charles Adam and Paul Tannery. 11 vols. (Paris: Vrin/CNRS, 1996) (AT).

the author after he has set out in the First Meditation the need to suspend judgement in everything that may be called into doubt. He has contemplated a radical sceptical scenario: that

> some malicious demon of the utmost power and cunning has employed all his energies in order to deceive me. I shall think that the sky, the air, the earth, colours, shapes and sounds and all external things are merely the delusions of dreams which he has devised to ensnare my judgement. I shall consider myself as not having hands or eyes, or flesh or blood or senses, but as falsely believing that I have all these things. (CSM ii. 15; AT vii. 22)

What is left is only the certainty of his own existence: for, no matter how powerful the deceiving demon is, as long as Descartes is contemplating his own deception, he himself, the meditating subject, must exist. Next Descartes addresses the question of what he is: whose existence is thereby demonstrated to be certain. He starts by reviewing his formerly held opinions on this matter. He had believed he was a man, and, accordingly, now he should investigate what man is. Saying that man is a rational animal offers no further enlightenment, for it only asks us to determine the difficult questions of what rational is, or what animal is. Instead he reflects that he had believed he had a body, and it further occurs to him that he was *nourished*, he did *move about*, he did *engage in sense perception* and *thinking*, and that he had referred all these actions to the soul.

Considering the definition of man as 'rational animal' is a clear reference to Aristotle, whose influence on philosophy of mind (and on much else) throughout the medieval period was decisive. The conception of a human being considered next is the Aristotelian conception inherited through the Scholastic tradition. A reminder of a few elements of the Aristotelian theory will be useful here.

In his major treatise on the soul, the *De Anima*, Aristotle proceeds in a way somewhat similar to Descartes's: before turning in earnest to the presentation of his own view, he devotes most of the first book to a review of his predecessors' opinions about the soul.

In the second book he sets out a systematic and more detailed presentation of his own view.

We resume our inquiry from a fresh starting-point by calling attention to the fact that what has soul in it differs from what has not, in that the former displays life. Now this word has more than one sense, and provided any one alone of these is found in a thing we say that thing is living. Living, that is, may mean *thinking* or *perception* or local *movement* and rest, or movement in the sense of *nutrition*, decay and growth. (*DA* II.2.413^{a}; emphasis added)[2]

In Aristotle's view, every living being has a soul, and the faculties associated with a living being form a hierarchy. The nutritive or vegetative faculty is basic: all living beings must possess it, and plants possess only this. The second order of living beings, animals, has sensory or perceptual faculties in addition; Aristotle thinks that every being capable of perception must possess at least the sense of touch, and possibly other senses besides. Sometimes the 'appetitive faculties' are mentioned separately; desire, passion, and wish belong here, and the view is that, if living beings have the sensory faculties, they must have the appetitive ones too (e.g. *DA* II.3.414^{b}). Certain kinds of animals also have the power of locomotion, and the ability to move also belongs to the sensory part. The next, third order of animate beings, human beings, has all the faculties listed so far, and also the power of thinking. Thinking includes the capacity of knowing, and of understanding, as well as that of theoretical and practical reasoning.

Descartes's list of what he used to believe the psychological faculties to be is precisely this Aristotelian list: nutritive, sensory, locomotive, and intellectual powers. These and a body constitute a man, according to the view Descartes had accepted before he embarked on his quest for certainty. Now he sets out to see what remains of his formerly held opinions after entertaining the radical

[2] References to Aristotle's work *De Anima* (*DA*) are to *On the Soul*, trans. J. A. Smith, in *The Complete Works of* Aristotle, ed. Jonathan Barnes, 6th printing with corrections, 2 vols. (Princeton: Princeton University Press, 1995).

doubt of the demon hypothesis, and finding unshakeable certainty in his own existence. Since it is part of the demon hypothesis that his body does not exist, this cannot serve as an answer to the question of 'What am I?'. Turning to the faculties associated with the soul, if it were true that my body did not exist, says Descartes, I could not walk or be nourished, and hence these could not belong to me. Neither would perception or sensation be possible: for perception presupposes the sense organs, and besides, Descartes remarks, we sometimes believe in our dreams that we perceive, when in reality we do not. Only the last psychological faculty survives scrutiny after the introduction of the demon hypothesis: even assuming that I am deceived by the demon, by entertaining this very hypothesis, I find myself thinking, and in this I also find the guarantee of my existence.

From the Aristotelian list of nutritive, sensory, locomotive, and intellectual faculties of the soul, only the last is kept as the essential attribute of the mind. This is certainly a major difference, but, at this point, there could still be a way of reading Aristotle that would bring him closer to this conception. After all, Descartes and Aristotle seem to agree that what is *distinctive of human beings*, and *human souls*, when compared to the rest of the created—or sublunary—world is the capacity of *thinking*. We may also recall that, even though Aristotle thinks that the soul is the form of the living body, and hence tends to dismiss the question of whether soul and body are distinct as unnecessary or meaningless (*DA* II.1.412^{b}5), in some passages he seems to allow that the thinking part alone may after all be separated from the body (*DA* II.5.430^{a}). This aspect of Aristotle's theory is notoriously difficult to interpret, but, nonetheless, it indicates that the distinctively human aspect of the soul, thinking, stands apart from the other psychological faculties—for example, in bearing a different relation to the body. However, when we turn to Descartes's explanation of what 'thinking' is, it becomes clear that their apparent agreement that thinking is the distinctive feature of the human soul or mind in fact conceals significant differences.

1.3 Varieties of Thought

We followed the argument in the Second Mediation to the point where Descartes introduces the demon hypothesis, finds certainty in his own existence, reviews his formerly held views about what he was, and, out of the Aristotelian list of the faculties of the soul—nutrition, movement, sense perception, thinking—retains only thought as truly belonging to him. Descartes now turns to the question of *what* a thinking thing is. His answer is: 'A thing that doubts, understands, affirms, denies, is willing, is unwilling, and also imagines and has sensory perceptions' (CSM ii. 19; AT vii. 28).

The last item on this list may be surprising: have we not already discarded perception as something whose functioning was called into doubt by the demon hypothesis, and hence which cannot truly belong to the self? Certainly, but it turns out that Descartes introduces a notion of perception that is somewhat different from the one employed before.

> it is also the same 'I' who has sensory perceptions, or is aware of bodily things as it were through the senses. For example, I am now seeing light, hearing a noise, feeling a heat. But I am asleep, so all this is false. Yet I certainly *seem* to see, to hear, and to be warmed. This cannot be false; what is called 'having a sensory perception' is strictly just this, and in this restricted sense of the term is simply thinking. (CSM ii. 20; AT vii. 29)

Perception, as understood earlier, required the sense organs and also that the objects of perception be real. This is clear from the reasons Descartes gave for *not* including perception among the faculties that belong to him essentially. He argued that, if he has no body, then he possesses no sense organs, and that, if the demon deceives him—or he is asleep—the objects of his perceptions do not exist either. The notion of perception, as newly introduced here, dispenses with both features. First, Descartes says that perceiving is being aware—or 'apprehending' in other translations—of objects *as it were* by the sense organs ('ego sum qui sentio, sive qui res corporeas *tanquam per sensus* animadverto' (AT vii. 29; emphasis added)). Secondly, even if the objects of perceptions turn out to be unreal, something still remains—namely the fact that it *seems* to us that we perceive them. Perceiving or having a sensory perception—or what we may call today 'having a perceptual experience'—in this new 'strict' sense is something I can have even if I am deceived by the demon. And, once we restrict the sense of 'perception' in this way, it turns out to be a variety of thinking—where the category of thought is understood to include all mental features, and not only the more limited class we usually mean by 'thought' in contemporary terminology.

We can see how these considerations shed light on 'the nature of the human mind', as it is promised in the title of the Second Meditation. What survives the demon hypothesis is the certainty of my existence as a thinking thing, or as a creature with a mind. Among the various activities of properties that characterize me, what counts as a variety of thought—that is, as a mental feature—is what I can claim to possess even on the assumption that I am deceived by the demon. Therefore sensory perception understood as the activity of my bodily sense organs is discarded; but sensory perception understood as a conscious event is retained. I shall argue that the remarkable feature of this procedure is that it gives exactly the results that match our contemporary conception of what belongs to the mind and what does not. Before a more precise assessment of this 'demon test' in the next section, let us see how some further items on the Aristotelian list of psychic faculties fare on the test.

If we look at Descartes's list of the activities of thinking things, we can notice something like a momentary hesitation before the last two items: 'and *also* imagines and has sensory perceptions'. This may be explained by the fact that, while the other activities are traditionally assigned to the rational part of the soul, imagination, together with perception, belongs to the sensory part in Aristotle's classification. But, supposing that I am deceived by the demon, would it still be possible to imagine, say, the space enclosed by the five sides of a pentagon? It certainly seems so; hence there is no surprise that we find imagination on Descartes's list.

What about sensations like pain or hunger? Aristotle classifies these too with the sensory part of the soul, and, as all sensory powers, they always involve some bodily activity. In fact, Descartes also believes that, as things are actually arranged with human beings, hunger or pain is always accompanied by a characteristic physiological process. But would it nonetheless be possible to have hunger or pain *in some sense* even if I were deceived by the demon, and had no body? I think the answer we may expect from Descartes is that, even if my body did not exist, and hence nor would my arm where I feel pain, nor my brain where the nerves normally carry the impulses from a bodily part that is hurt, it is still certain that it *seems* to me that I feel pain. Properly understood, this is what we may 'strictly' call having a sensation or an experience, and, as such, it is also a variety of thinking—that is, it belongs to the mind.[3]

Yet another example is provided by the emotions. These again are assigned to the sensory part by Aristotle, and therefore tied to some bodily activity (*DA* I.1.403^{ab}). And, once more, Descartes also identifies certain physiological processes as the characteristic accompaniments of emotions (or passions): these consist in certain motions of the blood, of the animal spirits, and of various organs of the body (as explained in detail in the *Passions of the Soul*). Now would it still be possible to feel joy even if one were deceived by the demon? The expected answer is that it would indeed; for, even

[3] It may be objected that Descartes claims, at least at one point (in a letter to More, August 1649), that 'the human mind separated from the body does not have sense-perception strictly so-called' (CSMK 380; AT v. 402). I think this claim, when properly understood, is not in tension with the claim that sensory perceptions, sensations, and the like are purely mental, and would exist also if I were deceived by the demon. Briefly, for a large class of mental features, which includes perceptions, sensations, emotions, memory, and imagination—what he calls 'the special modes'—Descartes believes that their direct and most proximate cause is always outside the individual mind. This extra-mental cause is usually the body, and, since every event needs a cause, the removal of the body would apparently result in the disappearance of these mental features. However, God or the demon can also occupy this role. For the details of the argument for this interpretation, see Farkas (2005).

if my body did not exist, and nor did my heart to pump blood faster when I feel joy, it is still certain that I am the same being who seems to have this feeling, and, once we see that this is what an emotion is, properly understood, it turns out to be yet another variety of thinking or mental episode.

Doubting, affirming, willing, imagining, having sensations, perceptions, and emotions pass the test, and hence turn out to be varieties of thought—that is, mental features. In contrast, having hands, digesting, eating, and moving do not pass the test, and hence turn out to be non-mental features. A note of warning here. In the examples above, we apparently found that mental activities could occur without their *characteristic physiological accompaniment*. But this, as we shall see below, does not entail that mental is distinct from the physical. I address this question briefly in the next section, and also in Sections 2.1 and 3.2; in the meantime, I simply ask the reader to keep in mind that the demon test is not, in itself, intended to commit us to dualism.

1.4 Incorporeal Minds and Certainty

The aim of this section and the next is to get a more precise idea of what is involved in the 'demon test'. In doing this, I shall rely on the *Meditations*, but my interest is not primarily historical. I cannot claim that what follows is the most faithful interpretation of Descartes, and, in fact, there will be explicit departures from the Cartesian theory on a number of points. The aim is to find the most plausible understanding of what I take to be Descartes's fundamental insight.

I start off with the thought that we can attribute various activities and properties to ourselves. For example: I am a woman, 5 ft 1 in. tall, a city-dweller, I got up at seven this morning, I run regularly, I like Thai food, I paint, yesterday I was thinking about the argument from illusion, I would like to learn Latin, and at the moment I have a slight pain in my knees (probably from all that running). Ontologically speaking, these attributions indicate *states*

I am in, or *events* I participate in, or *processes* I undergo, or *functions* I execute, or *dispositions* or *abilities* or simply *properties* that I have. I do not want to enter into any ontological dispute concerning the existence and nature of these categories; I shall mostly refer to any and all of these as 'features', and ask the reader to supply it with her favourite theory of basic ontological categories.

There is hardly a limit to the features I can attribute to myself, since my relational properties possibly include a description of the whole world in a Leibnizian fashion. I am interested in the following question: which of my activities and properties, and the events I participate in, do we consider as *mental* features? If one asks *why* it is important to distinguish mental features from others, this is a question I shall consider in Chapter 3. But for the moment, I am just going to assume that we have a more or less convergent idea of which features are mental and which are not, and that it is worth trying to find out what underlies this classification. The idea is that the demon test helps to achieve precisely this.

A word of clarification about the nature of this project. When I am talking about a 'test', I do not mean much more than a test—that is, the purpose of the following considerations is *not* to give some sort of non-circular or reductive analysis of the notion of 'mind', nor to explain the difference between the mental and the non-mental in terms that do not already rely on our understanding of these notions. The aim is really just to answer Rorty's charge that the items on the list of mental features do not really have a unifying mark, but are simply found there because of the contingencies of a certain tradition. I would like to argue that there is such a mark, even if it cannot be the basis of a reductive analysis.

Here is the first attempt to reconstruct exactly what happens in the demon test. Normally, I attribute to myself all sorts of properties. Then I assume that I am deceived by an evil demon, and there is no sky, no earth, I have no body, and so on. Then I see which properties I can still attribute to myself, and conclude that these properties belong to me as a thinking thing. It seems that these are the properties that I could have, even if no corporeal world—including my own body—existed. Then presumably the way to have them is by having them realized in an immaterial mind—or, if someone does not favour thinking substances, then in a Humean bundle of immaterial events.

This is *not* the interpretation I would like to endorse. First, although many people can apparently entertain the possibility of their disembodied existence with ease, and dualism has been claimed to be part of our common-sense conceptual framework (see Bloom 2004), I myself have always found it quite difficult to imagine that I could exist without my body. Perhaps this is just a personal limitation, so I do not want to put too much weight on it. But, more importantly, I wish to remain neutral on the question of physicalism. Physicalism can be held as a contingent doctrine: this is the view that everything, including the mind, is physical in this world, but disembodied minds are possible in other worlds. On this version, physicalism would be compatible with the claim that mental features are those that *could* be instantiated in an immaterial substance, even if they are *actually* instantiated by physical things. But, as is well known, Kripke (1972) and others have argued that physicalism, if held, should be held as a doctrine of the *necessary* identity of mind and body. In this case, if physicalism is true, my mental properties could not be instantiated in an immaterial mind.

I do not wish to take sides on any of these questions; the conception of the mind defended in this book is intended to be, as far as I can see its consequences, compatible with either version of physicalism, as well as with anti-physicalism. I cannot exclude the possibility that anti-physicalist arguments can be built on this conception, but this would certainly require further arguments. So I do not wish to endorse the view that a mental feature is a feature that could be exemplified even if nothing corporeal existed. (There is a further problem with this view, unconnected to physicalism, that I shall explain below.)

Here is the second attempt to capture the essence of the demon test. This time we locate the distinguishing characteristic of mental features not in a *metaphysical* dependence claim (that is, their independence of the existence of corporeal things), but rather in our *psychological* or *epistemic* attitudes towards these features. Gareth B. Matthews (1977: 68), for example, in reconstructing the reasoning of the Second Meditation, suggests that Descartes's criterion for selecting the functions of the mind is 'that an entity cannot both perform one of those functions and also doubt that it is performing it'. One way to understand this is that, whenever I attribute to myself a mental feature, it is *psychologically impossible for me to doubt* that I have that feature (I shall consider another understanding below). I can doubt that I see light, in the sense of seeing, which would imply that the light is there; but I cannot doubt that I *seem* to see light.

However, this will not do as a test for mental features, for there are other properties I cannot doubt I have, even though they are arguably not mental properties: for example, that I exist, that I am here, that I am identical to myself, that I either weigh exactly one pound or I do not. These are not mental properties, because something that entirely lacked mental features, say a pebble, could exemplify them—it could exist, could be here, it is identical to itself, and it either weighs exactly one pound or it does not.

Actually, this point shows a further problem with the previous suggestion—that mental properties are those that an immaterial substance can have. At least two of these properties—that I exist, and that I am identical to myself—can also be exemplified by immaterial substances. So, apart from the issue of physicalism, this may be an additional reason to reject the idea that mental features are those that can be instantiated by an immaterial substance.

The psychological indubitability test would let through non-mental properties. On the other hand, the test would seem to exclude some mental properties, since it seems possible for people to doubt some of their mental properties—for example, one may doubt whether one still loves someone, when a sudden threat of loss reveals that in fact one does.

In the last few paragraphs I have considered the suggestion that the demon hypothesis rules out the properties I am not certain that I possess, and I have interpreted certainty as psychological indubitability. 'Certainty' can also be understood as *guaranteed correctness*; an *epistemic*, rather than a psychological predicament (and this is probably closer to Descartes's own conception of certainty). But the attempt to use this understanding of certainty to establish the distinctive characteristic of mental features founders on the same examples as the previous understanding. I am in an excellent epistemic position with respect to my judgements that I exist, that I am here, that I am identical to myself, and that I either weigh exactly one pound or I do not. These examples show that there are non-mental features I can attribute to myself with guaranteed correctness. On the other hand, people may be wrong in their judgements in the kind of cases I cited above: for example, whether they love someone or not. (I shall discuss these cases in Chapter 2 in more detail.)

Our task in this section is to get a clearer idea of the demon test—the procedure that disqualifies nutrition and movement from the list of mental features, but includes thoughts, emotions, and perceptual experiences. I considered three candidates for the distinguishing characteristic of mental features. The first was that mental features can be exemplified even if nothing corporeal existed; I decided not to endorse this, because it may be incompatible with certain versions of physicalism. The second and third were two interpretations of the claim that the possession of mental features is believed with certainty, where certainty meant first psychological indubitability, then guaranteed correctness. On both interpretations, we found cases where possession of a *non*-mental feature *is* believed with certainty, and where possession of a mental feature *is not* believed with certainty. Let me present a different suggestion then.

1.5 Special Access

The protagonist of the *Meditations* is a reflective, enquiring, thinking subject. She sets out to investigate, to the best of her abilities, what can be known, what is there, what we are, and questions like that. The demon's intervention reduces the world to the enquiring subject. In my understanding, the role of the demon hypothesis is not to reduce the world to an incorporeal subject, but rather to reduce the world to *a unique centre of enquiry*: to *a subjective viewpoint* (and whether this needs corporeal existence or not is an open question). What survives the introduction of the demon hypothesis is the subject, and the portion of reality that is uniquely revealed from the subject's point of view.

As I see it, the line of thought leading to the conclusion of the Second Meditation is a systematic assessment of our cognitive faculties—that is, faculties that supposedly enable us to get to know things. One by one these faculties, and the subject matter they inform us about, are set aside, and what remain are the events or facts that are accessed by a certain cognitive faculty that places the subject in an exclusive position. This faculty is usually called reflection or introspection. Reflection is special in that its subject matter—that is, the facts known by reflection—can be known *in this way* only by the reflecting subject; they can be known by others only by using a different cognitive faculty. As we shall see in a moment, this is not true for other faculties and their subject matters. The first approximation of formulating the characteristic feature of the mind (as brought out by the demon test) is this: whatever can be known by the subject in a way it can be known by no one else belongs to the mind.

The starting point of my argument is the hope that my readers can recognize in themselves the phenomenon I am talking about. You can invoke the phenomenon by a simple exercise: for example, focus on the tactile experience you have through your left index finger at the moment. This is a kind of experience, a mental feature, that you can, and hopefully did, get to know. Now focus your attention on the question whether you have the intention of visiting the North Pole in the next two days. Hopefully you can acquire knowledge of this matter too. And now consider the question of how you could learn what other readers of this book (assuming that there are any) learnt about themselves when they were asked this question. If you are anything like me, then it will be clear that you cannot learn about their mental states in the way you did about your own. And, assuming that we are all similar in this respect, this means that they cannot learn about your mental states in the way you did. That this is fundamentally compelling is the basis of my argument.

Let me offer a reconstruction of the line of thought that leads to the above suggestion about the mental. As Descartes notes at the beginning of the *Meditations*, much of what we learn about the world we learn through the senses. The kinds of things I can learn through my senses are available to other potential knowers with a similar sensory apparatus, through the same route. I can get to know that the Eiffel tower is square by looking, and so can you. The demon takes away all knowledge of this kind. On the usual understanding—which is certainly supported by Descartes's formulations—the demon hypothesis involves the assumption that I do not possess a body at all (not even a brain). As I said, I am not sure that we can, or need, to make this assumption. But it is certainly part of the hypothesis—and, in my view, sufficient for the purposes of the argument—that I do not have sense organs, or that they stop functioning properly. This means that the sensory perceptions are not connected properly to the world any longer. Perceptual knowledge and its subject matter are consequently put aside.

Descartes does not consider testimony as a separate source of knowledge, but it will be instructive to see how it fares on the present issue. The kind of things I can learn through testimony can be learnt by others in the same way. I can get to know whether it is raining today in Copenhagen by reading it in the paper, and so can you. We should then expect that judgements arrived at on the basis of testimony are also suspended.

Consider next a priori knowledge of mathematics. In contemporary discussions of scepticism, the demon hypothesis is often replaced by the brain-in-a-vat hypothesis (e.g. Putnam 1981). In this version, we imagine that we are no more than a brain, placed in a vat containing nutrient fluids, our nerve endings connected to a supercomputer that feeds us with a perfect hallucination of the world we think we inhabit. There is an interesting difference between the demon and the brain-in-a-vat hypothesis though: while both make knowledge through the senses impossible—by simply obliterating our sense organs, or by suspending their proper connection to the environment—they potentially assign different status to knowledge of mathematics. In the usual versions, the brain-in-a-vat hypothesis does not make mathematical knowledge doubtful, nor does it question our intellectual reasoning abilities in general. It is a remarkable fact though that, in the First Meditation, it is at least contemplated that the demon's deceptive powers extend to mathematical truths: how do I know, Descartes asks, that I am not deceived each time I add together two and three?[4]

Knowledge of mathematics is similar to perceptual knowledge in that the kind of things I can learn about mathematics with the help of my reasoning faculties are available to other potential knowers endowed with a similar reasoning apparatus, through the same route. I can prove Pythagoras's theorem by using my reasoning abilities, and so can you. If the demon hypothesis asks us to set aside mathematics and its subject matter too, then another area is gone to which I do not have special access. (A note: contrary to a fairly widespread custom, I do not classify introspection as a variety of a priori knowledge. More on this in the next section.)

What is next? When Descartes raises the possibility that he is deceived about mathematics, he also mentions that he may be deceived about how many sides a square has. A priori knowledge of conceptual truths—like a square having four sides—is similar to the previously discarded faculties and their subject matters: other potential knowers, endowed with similar reasoning capacities, can

[4] See CSM ii. 14; AT vii. 21. Actually, this question is raised before the demon is introduced, at the stage when Descartes wonders if God could deceive him. The doubts concerning mathematics then do not always recur in the subsequent formulations of the demon hypothesis.

get to acquire them in the same way as I can. Since this cognitive faculty and what it reveals are not specifically related to the existence and identity of the subject in the way introspection and its subject matter are, we should put it aside, together with its subject matter.

Here I better issue a warning about the difference between using the demon hypothesis as a device in the sceptical argument, and using it as a device to establish the list of mental phenomena. Descartes's intention is probably to do the first, and mine is certainly the second, so I have to apologize for appropriating the device for my own purposes.

If the demon is used as a device in the sceptical argument, and we allow the demon's deceptive powers to extend to our a priori reasoning capacities concerning simple conceptual truths, we take a dangerous step. If I may go wrong even in thinking that, say, a square has four sides, then this seems to undermine the credibility of the very capacities that are needed to make any progress in the project of the *Meditations*. If my simple reasoning capacities are unreliable to this extent, then there is no point in meditating about them—or indeed about anything—any further, because meditation itself becomes pointless. In fact, we should become suspicious even about the road travelled so far: why should we pay any attention to the reasoning of the sceptical argument, if reasoning itself is subject to general doubt? Total scepticism is self-destructive, since it subverts both the sceptical reasoning and its promised antidote, and reduces us to mental inaction. Therefore I do not think it advisable to bring this consideration into the epistemological project, or, if we do, we should proceed with extreme care. On the whole, I wish to dissociate myself from Descartes's general epistemological views, and his attempt to deal with scepticism. I agree with those who say that, once the sceptical challenge is allowed to rise in its full-blown form, it becomes virtually impossible to answer. It is better not to allow the challenge to arise.

This means that the demon test cannot be used quite straightforwardly for my purposes: we cannot simply say that mental properties are precisely those that I can attribute to myself, even on the assumption that I am deceived by the demon. We have already seen how this straightforward application becomes problematic on some interpretations of what being deceived by the demon involves (that is, disembodied existence or limited certainty). The interpretation I am considering now—that introducing the demon discards some cognitive capacities and their subject matter, and keeps others—does not work straightforwardly either, because I have to assume that I keep my reasoning abilities even after the introduction of the demon, and reasoning capacities teach us about non-mental features as well. So the demon is only a suggestive device, because it helps us to focus on the subject's point of view.

Let me state again what the problem is. My proposal is that *the mental realm is nothing but the subject matter of the cognitive capacity that endows me with special access*: that is, the area that is known by me in a way that it is known by no one else. The fact that conceptual truths are *not* known in this way is consistent with this suggestion: that a square has four sides is not a feature of my mind. (Of course, what *I mean* by 'square' and 'four' and 'side' is such that the statement comes out true, and what I mean is a feature of my mind; but then it seems to me that this *is* something I know through special access.) The discrepancy is elsewhere: in that it is false that introspection is the *only* reliable cognitive faculty left after the introduction of the demon hypothesis. So the hitch is not in the thesis itself, but in the suggestion that the demon hypothesis exactly delivers the thesis. It is a shame, but I do not see how it can be helped. I cannot assume myself to be a creature without fundamental reasoning capacities and then see what else I could learn. But, if we only keep this point in mind, we can use the demon test to establish the list of mental phenomena.

Now while I am at it, I may as well admit another discrepancy. A cognitive faculty we have not considered is memory. Memory is an easy victim of sceptical doubts; the world could have come to exist five minutes ago, and so most things I believe on the basis of memory may be false. How does memory fare from the point of view of endowing the subject with special access? Here the answer does not seem to be unequivocal. There are things I can know through memory—for example, that it was raining yesterday—that are knowable by others in the same way: obviously, others too can remember that it was raining yesterday. There are other things though—for example, the fact that I was annoyed with myself for not taking an umbrella, which I can apparently recall in a way others cannot. (To be clear: the object of knowledge is not my present state of seeming to remember that I was annoyed, but rather my past state of being annoyed yesterday.)

If we go by the general spirit of the demon hypothesis, there is no reason to think that beliefs gained from memory survive the intervention of the demon. Yet, if what I just said is right, then there is a use of memory that seems to endow the subject with special access. My response is as before. The thesis that special access reveals the mental is consistent with this finding—for what I recall through special access in the previous example is how I *felt* about something, and that is a mental feature. But, alas, we have to register a further problem with the idea that what is left after the demon's appearance is exactly the cognitive faculties that provide special access. Reflection is usually taken to be the ability to gain knowledge of my present mental states. But it is natural to think that similar knowledge can be extended to my past mental states: reflective memory of my past beliefs or feelings will provide special access to its subject matter.

The upshot is that the kind of things I know perceptually, or a priori, or through testimony, and, in some cases, through memory, can be known by others through the same routes, respectively. But what I learn by reflection or introspection can be learnt in that way only by me. What belongs to the mind can be determined relative to this capacity: the subject matter of this faculty is the mind.

We can conceive this thesis as creating a notion analogous to the notion of observable properties, which are also understood relative to a cognitive capacity: observable properties are those properties we can get to know through unaided perception. The thesis here is that mental properties are the specially accessible properties. The analogy is not meant to extend further than the proposal that some properties are defined relative to a cognitive faculty; I am not suggesting the observation model of introspection (accounting for the nature or structure of our introspective faculty lies beyond the scope of this book). On the other hand, the analogy could also show that the fact that a property is determined relative to a certain cognitive capacity does not mean that the capacity in question is *infallible* or *omniscient*. Observation is neither infallible nor omniscient about observational properties; similarly, introspection is neither infallible nor omniscient about introspectible properties. As I noted earlier, there are cases where we are mistaken about our mental features; so introspection, just like other cognitive faculties, is both restricted and fallible. At the same time, we should expect that introspection has a default epistemic primacy over the domain of introspection.

A final aspect of the analogy is that observation is not exclusive to observable properties; we can learn about these matters, for example, through testimony. Similarly, there is no reason to exclude the possibility that the mental features that are available to special access can also be known in some other way.

1.6 Cognitive Faculties

The picture I am offering is based on the conviction that it makes good sense to classify our knowledge gathering and retaining activities into basic cognitive faculties—or into 'ways of knowing'—on the basis of what we can say about the subject matter, or the mechanism, or the nature of warrant attached to, or the phenomenology or ontology of, these faculties. For example, though I absolutely lack the space to argue for this here, I believe that a priori reasoning is a way of knowing that is different from sense perception (for some arguments, see Bonjour 1998). I also believe that memory is distinct from sense perception, and it provides a distinctive way of acquiring knowledge. Bodily awareness—including proprioception, interoception, kinaesthesia—is yet another cognitive faculty. And I would like to claim that introspection is a *sui generis* way of acquiring knowledge, which is distinct from the previous capacities, and that the specific feature of introspection is that it is the only asymmetrical capacity, in the sense already canvassed: it alone provides special access to its subject matter. (In Section 2.1, I shall come back to the question of why knowledge of our body through bodily awareness is different from introspective knowledge.)

In the discussions about self-knowledge and externalism—a topic that is very relevant to my project and that will be extensively discussed in the second part of this book, mainly in Chapter 6—self-knowledge is often classified as a form of a priori knowledge. The issue is, of course, to some extent terminological; if, for example, 'a priori' simply meant 'not through sense perception', then it would be plausible to say that introspection was a priori. However, there is also a substantial point: since, throughout this book, I use the term 'a priori' to mean the kind of knowledge we have of logic, mathematics, and conceptual truths, and since I think that introspective knowledge is importantly different from these kinds of knowledge, I do not think it is helpful to classify introspection in the same category. (I shall consider the issue of externalism and self-knowledge in Chapter 6, where I hope to take into account various views on this issue discussed in the contemporary literature. The following discussion, though related, focuses mainly on the interpretation of the demon test.)

A priori knowledge (that is, the kind of knowledge we have of logic, maths, and conceptual truths) is traditionally regarded as knowledge attained by the use of reason alone, and this description does not seem to apply to knowledge of our mental states (cf. Nuccetelli 1999). When I register that I feel a slight pain in my knee, the faculty I am using is different from the one used in establishing the correctness of the *modus ponens*. One difference between introspection and a priori knowledge is precisely that introspection provides special access to its subject matter, while a priori knowledge does not. It is worth noting that even philosophers who are sceptical about a priori knowledge of a traditional kind, like Donald Davidson, recognize that introspection has a certain essential first-person aspect. I do not share Davidson's scepticism about a priori knowledge, but I think his example supports the claim that introspection should not be categorized together with the kind of a priori knowledge we have of logic and mathematics.

I am now going to discuss a few examples that are relevant both to the distinction between a priori knowledge and introspection, and to the outcome of the demon test. In Section 1.4, I considered and rejected the suggestion that the mark of mental features is that they are psychologically indubitable or epistemically certain. One reason for the rejection was that some apparently non-mental features have this characteristic. The first group of these features contain what we may call 'logically evident properties'—for example, that I either weigh exactly one pound or I do not, or that I am identical to myself. These are good examples of properties I know I have a priori; one plausible suggestion is that these statements are analytic, so I can know their truth just on the basis of understanding their meaning. (It is, of course, a further question, and a very difficult one, whether all a priori truths are analytic.) Everyone who is endowed with the capacity of analytic or a priori reasoning will know, in the same way as I do, that I possess these properties. My own proposal avoids the difficulty the other suggestions faced: since I do not have special access to the fact that I either weigh one pound or not, this property will not figure on the list of mental properties, according to my theory.

There is another group of features that caused a problem for the psychological indubitability and epistemic certainty theories, and this group is a lot more tricky. Here we find knowledge of facts like the following:

(E) I exist

(H) I am here

These are psychologically indubitable and epistemically certain, and yet, as I remarked earlier, they do not seem to have much to do with the mind: existing or being somewhere are properties that a being without any psychology could possess. Now the reason they are tricky is that these features seem to pass even my version of the demon test: for, apparently, I know that I exist or that I am here in a way no one else does. Other people learn of my existence through experience, but my own justification for the claim that I exist is not empirical. In fact, I am uniquely placed to gain certain knowledge of my own existence.

However, there are some important differences between knowledge of (E) and (H), on the one hand, and knowledge of my mind through introspection, on the other—as, for example, Paul Boghossian (1989) argued. The striking feature of (E) and (H) is that they are *contextually self-verifying*: every time they are thought, they are true. Our justification for them, or our inability to doubt them, comes from this feature. To be more precise, the justification seems to arise from two circumstances: first, that all thought episodes expressed by (E) or (H) are true; secondly, that we *recognize* that this is the case. This latter part is the cognitive achievement we perform in acquiring these pieces of knowledge, and the faculty that we apply in this achievement is not introspection, but reason. It is the kind of justification we can all figure out—for example, for each tokening of the sentence 'This sentence is true', or each utterance of the sentence 'An utterance is made'. And there does not seem to be much of a privileged access in the way of our getting to know these latter examples.

Now compare this with my introspective knowledge of my desire to learn Latin, or of the slight sensation of pain in my knee. Clearly, the thoughts expressed as

(D) I desire to learn Latin
(P) I feel a slight pain in my knee

are not contextually self-verifying; I could easily entertain these thoughts without their being true (in fact, since I wrote down these examples in Section 1.4, the pain has gone, so at the moment I am entertaining (P) without its being true). My justification for these claims on the occasions where they form knowledge is, therefore, not coming from their contextually self-verifying nature and my reasoning about this. Instead, it is coming from an application of my ability to detect some of my features in a special way—that is, by introspection.

Introspection, as I said earlier, is by no means an infallible capacity; it is not only that I could entertain (D) and (P) without their being true, but I could also falsely believe them. Admittedly, circumstances in which I falsely believe (P) have to be rather extreme, but I think that one can find such circumstances. This points to a further interesting difference between these cases and cases like (E) and (H): no one could falsely believe (E) and (H). However, this is not a sign of some superior cognitive faculty working here: the guaranteed truth of each episode of thinking (E) or (H) is not a cognitive achievement at all; it does not seem to come from an application of any particular cognitive ability. It is true that my *knowledge* of (E) and (H) does require some reasoning, but the truth of each episode of (E) and (H) is guaranteed, even if I never complete the requisite cognitive achievement.

So, even though, at first sight, the facts that I exist, and that my knee does not hurt now, are all known by me in a way known by no one else, this asymmetry has different sources in the two types of cases. In one case, the source is the contextually self-verifying character of the thought, which, in itself, does not have much to do with any cognitive achievement; in the other, it is the application of a faculty that provides privileged, though fallible, access to its subject matter. My proposal is that we identify the mental as the realm we get to know through the exercise of introspection, which is the only cognitive faculty that provides privileged access to its subject matter. Since knowledge that I exist or that I am here is not achieved through introspection, these features should not be classified as mental.

One more remark on this issue. There is knowledge—the kind of knowledge I call 'a priori'—which is achieved by the application of reason alone, without the help of, say, introspection or perception. But it seems to me that virtually all knowledge involves some use of reason; even acquisition of empirical or introspective knowledge relies on a background ability to make simple inferences or to keep in mind conceptual connections. One activity in which the application of reason and introspection are inextricably mixed is conceptual analysis. For example, when I started to work on the topic of epistemic discriminability—which is the focus of Chapter 5—I realized that I use the term 'discriminate' in at least three different senses. Distinguishing these meanings was a result of reason revealing that certain commitments about the use of the term were incompatible, and an introspective realization that, in different contexts, I have these commitments because of what I mean by the word.

Let me emphasize again that I am not trying to give some sort of reductive analysis of the mental; clearly, introspection itself is a mental activity—which is evident from the fact that I can introspect my acts of introspection—so, in trying to explain what belongs to the mind, I have to rely on a prior understanding of what certain mental activities involve. However, I trust that the proposal is not trivial; if I meant by 'introspection' simply the faculty that enables us to know our mental features, then it would be a tautology that the mental realm is the introspectible realm. What gives content to my view is the claim that introspection is the only cognitive faculty that provides privileged access to its subject matter. That is, what you get to know by the use of this faculty is something that cannot be known to anyone through the use of the same faculty. If someone did not know what the mind was, I could not really use this idea to explain it to her; what I am hoping is that my readers are all familiar with what the mind is by having one, by knowing one, and that they recognize in themselves the working of this special faculty I am pointing out.

1.7 The Subject's Point of View

The suggestion presented so far is by no means new: the idea that privileged access is the mark of the mental, or that the mind is essentially revealed from the subject's point of view, has been both defended and criticized before. When talking about the special nature of self-knowledge, a whole variety of features tends to be mentioned, often without especially distinguishing them; that self-knowledge is a priori, privileged, infallible, authoritative, that its subject matter is private, and so on (see, e.g., Ludlow and Martin 1998: 1). And even these notions are understood in different ways by different people; for example, Ronald de Sousa (2002) distinguishes twelve varieties of subjectivity, all of which have been claimed to play an important role in the characterization of the mental.

To be clear, let me indicate a few senses of subjectivity that I do *not* want to endorse. I do not suggest that mental states are 'owned' in a special way; my understanding of subjectivity is essentially epistemic, in the sense that it relies on a certain cognitive capacity (for an exposition and a convincing criticism of the special 'ownership' view, see Tye 1995). I do not suggest that the mind is 'private' in the sense that no one else could ever know what goes on in my mind; other people can learn very well about my mental states, albeit not by introspection. Nor do I suggest that introspection is privileged in the sense that it is infallible, incorrigible, or omniscient. Introspection, like all our cognitive capacities, is a useful but imperfect device. And, as I said above, I do not want to classify introspection as a priori in the same sense as knowledge of mathematics or logic is a priori.

It may seem strange that some portion of reality is knowable by one person in this special way. An explanation of this circumstance is offered by the observation that mental facts are perspectival facts. To be a subject is to possess a point of view. For a minded being, things do not just surround one, but they appear to one in a certain way, they feel in a certain way, they are enjoyed or they fill one with despair, things are desired or doubted or believed. This perspective includes not only the world around us, but also ourselves. There is a certain way for me to be when I am cold or when I am hot, when I am at ease or when I am worried. Only a creature capable of having a point of view can be engaged in such a fact. Things simply surround a church tower or a mountain top; but there is no such thing as how things are *for* the church tower.

Some of the minded beings are endowed with a special capacity of acquiring knowledge about these perspectival facts. When this happens, we can expect the subject to have prima facie authority over others in these matters: since the very nature of these facts is defined by their layout in a certain perspective, the subject whose perspective it is enjoys a uniquely revealing view of them. If there is a statue that shows a particular shape only when viewed from a certain direction, then the person who stands precisely in that direction is in the most favourable position to have that shape revealed to her. Things could go wrong: lightning might strike or darkness might descend, and so the shape might become invisible or distorted. It is also possible that others looking on from a different direction somehow work out how the statue would look from where the subject is standing. But still, being positioned in that very place will give a significant advantage to the subject's point of view. When the subject believes she has a mental feature, her view has initial warrant, and also a default authority over others. Perspectival facts are accessible in a privileged way.

My mind encompasses features that I can get to know in a way no one else can. The claim is made in the first person; the boundaries of *my* mind are given by what *I* know in a special way. I write these lines trusting that my readers are creatures quite similar to me; and, for each of us, what is given in this way will turn out to include pretty much the same list of mental phenomena.

There is, however, no guarantee that this will be the same for every conceivable creature. Not everyone has the kind of mind we do. Before I discuss the significance of what we find on our list of mental features, I need to consider some possible objections. This is the topic of the next chapter.

2

UNCONSCIOUS, CONSCIOUS, BODILY

2.1 Access to the Body

The conclusion of the previous chapter was that the distinguishing feature of my mind is that it is knowable by me in a way that is knowable to no one else. It may be objected that the same is true for my body: I can learn about my bodily states in a way no one else can. I said that reflection was the only asymmetrical cognitive faculty, but, the objection may continue, the same applies to bodily awareness. Bodily awareness includes proprioception, interoception, kinaesthesia, and it is a cognitive faculty distinct from sense perception (that is, perception through the five external sense organs). In searching for the mark of the mental, Richard Rorty (1970: 409, 413) summarily dismisses the candidates 'introspectibility' or 'special access', because, he claims, one has special access say to one's stomach fluttering or a vein throbbing in one's leg, but these are physical, and not mental events. A certain damage in the tissue of my body gives rise to the feeling of pain in me; other people may see the damage or learn about it in some other way, but no one else would learn about *my* bodily states through having this sensation.

I should hasten to add that (unlike Rorty) I am not assuming here that the experience itself is different from some or other bodily event. In fact, throughout this discussion, all we assume is a classification of our activities into the mental and the *non-mental*, or the mental and the *merely physical*. Rorty (1970: 402) would disagree, for he claims that 'it is part of the sense of "mental" that being mental is incompatible with being physical'. Rorty thinks that the remotest plausibility, or perhaps the very intelligibility of dualism, depends on conceiving the mental in this way, and, since we *can* make sense of dualism, the choice is obvious. There are two options on Rorty's scenario: either we think that mental properties exist, in which case we are, by definition, committed to some form of dualism; or alternatively, if we want to be materialists, it has to be the eliminativist version, which denies the existence of the mental altogether.

Having only these two choices would make most contemporary (non-eliminativist) versions of physicalism not so much false, but rather unintelligible. And it is not only the contemporary positions. Perhaps there is a use of 'mind' in the *Meditations* that *means* thinking, non-extended substance—understanding thinking substance as a substance whose essential attribute is thought, *as opposed* to extension. But I do not think there is any suggestion that the characteristic activities of such a substance—various mental phenomena—are to be understood as immaterial *by definition*. Hobbes, in his objections to the *Meditations*, allows that Descartes is right in attributing the faculty of thinking to himself, and inferring his existence, but not that this would entail that he is an immaterial substance. As he says: 'it may be that the thing that thinks is the subject to which mind, reason or intellect belong; and this subject may thus be corporeal. The contrary is assumed, not proved' (CSM ii. 122; AT vii. 173).

Descartes—who hasn't got much time for Hobbes in general—is not moved: 'But I certainly did not assume the contrary, nor did I use it as a "basis" of my argument. I left it quite undecided until the Sixth Meditation, where it is proved' (CSM ii. 123; AT vii. 175). If we agree that the activities of the 'mind, reason and intellect' are mental phenomena, this exchange would make no sense if 'mental' *meant* something incompatible with the physical or the corporeal. Hobbes could not claim that these activities may be corporeal, and Descartes could not claim that he leaves open the question of whether they are until the Sixth Meditation. Therefore I see no reason to adopt this understanding.

Accordingly, suppose that the distinction is drawn between the mental and the *mere* bodily, and we are considering the following objection. All cognitive faculties work through producing some appropriate mental states in us; for example, sense perception works by producing perceptual states, and, since these are appropriately connected to states of the world, they enable us to acquire knowledge about the world. Bodily awareness is a faculty that produces its characteristic mental events in the form of the bodily sensations of hunger, pain, a feeling of a vein throbbing, and so on. Since these are appropriately connected to various states of my body, I can learn about mere bodily events in my own body through having some specific mental events. Since no one else has bodily sensations produced by my body, this is a way to learn about my body in a way no one else can.

But this seems to me a practical, rather than a conceptual point. It seems it would be possible to establish a causal mechanism in which certain changes in my body would cause appropriate changes in someone else's nervous system or their brain, and would give rise to the corresponding feelings. Nikola Grahek (2001) describes cases where people who had lost the ability to feel pain in various parts of their body were given a 'substitute pain system'. The system was supposed to alert the subjects to potential damage in the insensitive parts of their bodies by giving them a mildly painful electric shock in another part of their body. These wires could also have been connected to another person, in which case the other person could have learnt about the damage in the first person's body through the sensation of pain.

A damage in my foot could cause a feeling of pain in someone else. But this would not mean that she felt *my* experience; the pain she felt would be felt as her own. Similarly, the fact that you and I look at the same object, and, through a similar mechanism in our perceptual system, have a visual experience caused by the same thing, would not mean that you have *my* visual experience when this happens. Seeing the same—that is, numerically the same—foot and 'hurting' the same foot would both be cases when our experiences have a common cause. The difference is, of course, that, as things are arranged with us, we often have similar causal impact from the same thing through our visual system, but not through the mechanism of producing bodily sensations.

It could still be objected that, if someone else had a sensation of pain caused by damage in *my* body, she would still not learn about the damage in the way I do: for it is characteristic of the feeling of pain that the *felt* location of pain is always in our own body. In the situation envisaged, if my foot as it were hurt someone else, it would feel to her as if the damage was done to *her* own body, but, since this would be wrong, she could not acquire knowledge about my body through sensations in the way I can. There is indeed a crucial link between the character of sensations and our conception of our own body. Descartes says in the Sixth Meditation:

> As for the body which by some special right I called 'mine', my belief that this body, more than any other, belonged to me had some justification. For I could never be separated from it, as I could from other bodies; and I felt all my appetites and emotions in, and on account of, this body; and finally, I was aware of pain and pleasurable ticklings in parts of this body, but not in other bodies external to it. (CSM ii. 52; AT vii. 76)

Similar lines from Locke:

> Thus, the limbs of his body are to every one a part of Himself; he sympathizes and is concerned for them. Cut off a hand, and thereby separate it from that consciousness he had of its heat, cold, and other affections, and it is then no longer a part of that which is himself, any more than the remotest part of matter. (Locke 1690: II.xxvii.11)

The fundamental idea of the body that 'by a special right' I call my own is the one with which I have the following intimate connection: I learn about its happenings through a specific class of sensations. I would add another element, not mentioned by Descartes: it is also the one I can control in a special way. I realize this may sound alarmingly dualist: as if I assumed that I first have an idea of myself as separate from my body, and then tried to find, among all the bodies around, which is precisely mine (like trying to find my own umbrella among all the others when leaving a restaurant). This is indeed implausible, but we do not *need* to think in this way; the idea is neutral with respect to dualism and monism. It may be that I *am* simply my body; I could still say that the fundamental conception of the *boundaries* of my own body is a result of the complex and systematic array of bodily sensations that have a felt location, and the similarly complex and systematic ways in which my intentions control the movements of parts of my body.

We all know how this goes in the normal case. Now I wonder what would happen if I found myself affected in the way my body normally affects me by something that I had not considered as belonging to my body hitherto. If this again sounds too suggestive of dualism, we can put it in another way: what would happen if I became aware of something I had not considered as part of my body, in the way I am normally aware of some part of myself, that is, of my body? We certainly cannot ignore the systematic and, on the whole, reliable occurrence of sensations in their role of delivering knowledge of our own body. If damage in someone else's body regularly caused a distinctive kind of pain sensation in me, and I became aware of this connection, then there is no reason why this should not become a way of acquiring knowledge. But how would it *feel*? It is hard to say. Maybe my conception of the boundaries of my body would be extended; or pain would assume more of the character of outer perception; or possibly it would remain an anomaly. In any case, it could be a source of knowledge.

So it is in principle possible for someone else to learn about the damage in my body through having a certain feeling, which is the way I learn about these things. But, as I said, this would not mean that they feel my pain. The pain they feel would express their perspective on things, not mine; it would be felt as theirs, and consequently it would be theirs. This means that they would not be able to learn about *my pain*—as opposed to the damage in my body—in the way I do.

It is worth noting that this line of thought fits well with the Cartesian conception of mind and body, and less so with the Aristotelian one. One of Descartes's departures from the Aristotelian conception, which he himself considers very significant, is the explanation of the physiological aspects of experiences in mechanical terms, as opposed to an explanation in terms of form and matter. When there is a certain impact on the surface of my body, say a fire close to my foot, the nerves leading from the foot to the brain forward a certain impulse, 'just as when you pull one end of a string, you cause a bell hanging at the other end to ring at the same time' (*Treatise on Man*, CSM i. 101; AT xi. 142). As Descartes notes (in the Sixth Meditation, CSM ii. 60; AT vii. 86 ff.), one could interfere with this process at any point; that is, as it were, pull the string at any point to sound the bell. To continue the metaphor, it would then in principle be possible to wire up things so that an impact on my foot would sound an alarm in your brain, and you would feel the pain. It is less obvious how we could make sense of this in the Aristotelian conception, and within the framework of soul relating to body as form to matter.

The examples discussed above offer further insight into how the mental is distinguished from the non-mental. Rorty unhesitatingly classifies the throbbing of a vein in one's leg as a physical—or, as I would say, a mere bodily—phenomenon, and naturally I agree. The *feeling* of a vein's throbbing is, of course, a mental phenomenon; the two are different, since a vein could throb without my feeling it, and, if there is such a thing as phantom pain, there could presumably be a phantom throbbing of a vein. The feeling of a vein's throbbing may be identical to another physical event—presumably some brain event—but not to the throbbing of the vein itself.

Certain sensations are identified with respect to a mere bodily occurrence: we say it is the feeling of a '...', where '...' stands for a mere bodily event, as in the case of the vein throbbing or the stomach fluttering. Others have their own distinctively mental word: pain is an example, or hunger. All these latter have in common the fact that they are essentially *felt*. Now it is a somewhat puzzling question why some sensations fall into one category rather than the other. For example, we lack almost entirely a vocabulary for distinctive mental expressions to describe the various sensations of our body's *moving* in a certain way. There is the *feeling* of walking, of falling, of my arms being raised, my muscles tightening, my legs being crossed, and so on. All these are described as a feeling of a certain *bodily event*, but, as with other feelings, they could occur independently of the bodily event that we use to identify them. One could have a feeling of walking even if in fact one was not walking, as Descartes famously points out in his reply to Gassendi's objection (CSM ii. 244; AT vii. 352; see also the quotation from the *Principles* in the next section). But there are almost no distinctively mental expressions for sensations of movements, possibly with the exception of sensations having to do with balance—such as dizziness or vertigo.

Here is an interesting hypothesis to consider. Suppose we did have a vocabulary of mental terms that denoted *sui generis* sensations of movements without reference to mere bodily events. In that case, perhaps 'movement' would be treated in a way somewhat similar to perception when it comes to the assessment of the Aristotelian psychic faculties. Maybe we would, analogously to perception, 'split' movement into two, distinguishing its merely physiological aspect on one side, and the sensation on the other. Since we lack such a vocabulary, sensations of movement are not listed as a separate kind of mental phenomena—they are classified simply among feelings or experiences, without reference to what they are experiences of.

2.2 Stream of Consciousness and Standing States

Another worry about the proposed list of mental features may be that it places undue emphasis on consciousness. In this section, I introduce the problem and attempt to answer it.

Mental features are customarily classified into two types. The first group includes occurrent events, with perceptual experiences and sensations as the typical examples. Consider my present visual experience of the computer screen and the feeling of the pleasant warmth of the spring weather: I am immediately aware of them, and I could not have such mental episodes without a similar accompanying awareness. I cannot say that I see, feel, or experience something now without it somehow impinging on my present state of consciousness.

Members of the second group are said to be best described as states rather than events, and various propositional attitudes are offered as examples. At this moment, I have numerous beliefs say about my past, and numerous intentions about my future, but I am not aware of them in the way I am aware of my present experiences; they do not impinge on my consciousness in the way mental episodes in the first group do. These standing states certainly have characteristic relations to some events in the stream of consciousness; for example, in my acts of deliberations, a reflection on my beliefs becomes a part of my stream of consciousness.

The relation between a standing state and the related conscious events is a matter of debate. According to one picture, propositional attitudes can enter and leave the stream of consciousness: my belief that I live in Budapest is not conscious most of the time; but right now, with the act of contemplation, it becomes conscious. For example, Freud (1915: 175) talks of a psychical act that is not conscious but is '*capable of becoming conscious*' (emphasis added). According to another position, the two types of features are fundamentally different in kind, and it makes no sense to speak of a conscious version of a belief; standing states are, by their nature, non-conscious, even though they may have manifestations in the stream of consciousness—for example, in the form of acts of judgements (Crane 2001: sect. 4.32, presents a convincing argument for this claim). It should be noted that, when we talk about beliefs not being conscious in this sense, this has nothing to do with repression or the Freudian unconscious, as the example of my generally non-conscious, but not at all repressed, belief that I live in Budapest shows. (See Section 2.3 below for a discussion of repressed mental states.)

In a systematic elaboration of his views in the *Principles of Philosophy*, Descartes offers the following definition of thought:

By the term 'thought', I understand everything which we are aware of as happening within us, in so far as we have awareness of it. Hence, thinking is to be identified here not merely with understanding, willing and imagining, but also with sensory awareness. For if I say 'I am seeing, or I am walking, therefore I exist' and I take this as applying to vision or walking as bodily activities, then the conclusion is not absolutely certain. This is because, as often happens during sleep, it is possible for me to think that I am seeing or walking, though my eyes are closed and I am not moving about; such thoughts might even be possible if I had no body at all. But if I take 'seeing' or 'walking' to apply to the actual sense or awareness of seeing and walking, then the conclusion is quite certain, since it relates to the mind, which alone has the sensation or thought that it is seeing or walking. (CSM i. 195; AT viiiA. 7)

The mental features that seem to fit this definition best are events in the stream of our consciousness. Indeed, it is a commonly accepted view that the modern philosophical tradition simply identifies the mind with consciousness; see, for example, the entry on consciousness in a standard reference work like the *Stanford Encyclopedia of Philosophy* (van Gulick 2004). Another classic modern author who is brought as an example is Locke. In his case the intent is even clearer (and, the original being written in English, the terminology is arguably closer to ours): 'consciousness... is inseparable from thinking, and, as it seems to me, essential to it: it being impossible for any one to perceive without perceiving that he does perceive. When we see, hear, smell, taste, feel, meditate, or will anything, we know that we do so' (Locke 1690/1975: II.xxvii.9). In the subsequent sections, Locke mentions that consciousness is interrupted by sleep, and this suggests that by 'consciousness' he does indeed mean the stream of consciousness. If this is so, then apparently both Descartes and

Locke (and presumably the majority of the modern philosophical tradition) rely on a definition of thought that leaves out a large part of what makes up our mentality. And, again, this does not mean only Freudian unconscious—which they possibly did ignore—but features that they themselves would have certainly regarded as belonging to the mind: say, our beliefs about the past, or our learning of mathematics that we do not presently entertain. Since I suggest adopting the Cartesian conception thought, this would be a very uncomfortable consequence for my theory.

One way to overcome the problem would be to follow the first of the two views mentioned above, according to which beliefs, desires, and other standing attitudes pass in and out of the stream of consciousness. The definition of thought would then include everything that *can* enter the stream of consciousness (see Searle 1983). However, I hesitate to choose this option, since I do not want to exclude the view that standing states are, by nature, non-conscious.

Let us revisit the moment when, after concluding that thinking is the only activity that survives the demon test, Descartes sets out to investigate what thinking is. We have already seen (in Section 1.3) how Descartes classifies sensory perceptions as certain kind of thoughts. A few sentences earlier, he says: 'Is it not the one and the same "I" who is now doubting almost everything, who nonetheless understands some things, who affirms that this one thing is true, denies everything else, desires to know more, is unwilling to be deceived... ' (CSM ii. 19; AT vii. 28). It is Descartes's present concern to sort out what he doubts, so perhaps we can say that doubting is part of his stream of consciousness. But the fact that he desires to know more, and that he is unwilling to be deceived, though momentarily called to mind, will obviously characterize him also a few pages later, when his attention is no longer focused on them. These are standing states. Yet Descartes has no more difficulty in recounting them as belonging to him than he has in recounting his present sensory perceptions a few sentences later. I think we can leave it open whether these desires themselves become conscious in these acts of reflection; we need to say only that Descartes becomes conscious of *having the desires* in question. The *reflective act* itself is part of the stream of consciousness, but its object may or may not be.

Since standing states and occurrent events differ in their nature, I suppose that the process by which we reflect upon them, and hence become conscious of having them, is different. What these processes look like, I cannot speculate here. Occurrent states, one may assume, lie closer to reflective access, since they already form part of the stream of consciousness. But, as Descartes's reflections—and our immediate understanding of what is involved in them, and our unhindered ability to execute such acts ourselves—show, we can easily extend our reflective attention to our standing states as well. It may not be evident how it is done, but it is certainly done.

It is clear from Descartes's, and especially from Locke's, words quoted above that the notion of consciousness they use is different from the one used at the beginning of this section, in introducing the distinction between two kinds of mental features. Many would agree that the consciousness that characterizes say perceptions is something that animals can possess. However, the same animals will not have the reflexive ability to learn that they possess these mental features: for example, they will, in all likelihood, lack the notion of a sensory perception that is required to form a belief that one has sensory perceptions. Consequently, they will also lack knowledge that they possess these states. But, as Locke makes clear, he thinks that the consciousness that essentially accompanies thoughts is something that implies *knowledge* that we have these thoughts.

Let us see where this leaves our present proposal. My mind is what is knowable for me in a way it is knowable to no one else. To activate this knowledge, a conscious act of reflection is required, in which the judgement that I possess one or another mental feature is formulated. This does not require that every mental feature is actually or potentially conscious, in the sense that consciousness is employed to characterize the mental features of the first group; what is required is only that they are available to conscious acts of reflection. When I reflect upon my belief that I live in Budapest, we need not assume that the belief itself is conscious; rather that I am conscious of having the belief.

Does this mean that creatures incapable of reflection, like most, or all, non-human animals, lack mental features altogether? The answer is 'no', and it had better be 'no', because it seems very plausible that non-human animals can have mental features: for example, perceptions, bodily sensations, desires, memories. It may seem that a theory that tries to capture the mark of the mental in something that is distinctively human, or that is distinctively ours, will face difficulties in understanding how non-human animals can also be in possession of mental features. For example, on Descartes's dualist conception—at least according to the most straightforward understanding—having a mind truly separates us from the rest of the created world, since we alone have immaterial souls. But the same move makes it impossible for animals to possess any mental features. (For a more subtle interpretation of Descartes's views, see Cottingham 1978.)

According to my proposal, anything we discover in ourselves by reflection belongs to the mind, and any creatures that have *any* of these—that feel, perceive, remember, think—count as having a mind, even if they themselves do not have the power of reflection. It is true that the demarcation of mental features happens from a distinctively human perspective; the mind is an anthropocentric, or rather a 'personocentric', notion, since classifying our features into mental and non-mental categories has a special significance for us, which I shall explain in Chapter 3. I do not think this classification has such a special significance for, say, cats. Cats engage in a number of characteristic activities: they are nourished, they move, they perceive, and they can probably perform simple cognitive tasks, but, as far as only cats are concerned, nothing much hangs on the question of which of these activities are mental. The classification of their activities is derivative from the classification of our activities. So, in my view, a lot of non-human animals have a mind, but not exactly the kind of mind we have, and hence—to refer ahead to the conclusion of Chapter 3—they are not persons.

2.3 The Mind as an Ideal

But even if we can dispel the worry that non-conscious mental features are not part of the mind on the Cartesian conception, there remains a problem about *unconscious* states. As we saw, there are mental states we possess that need not be part of our stream of consciousness, but we can easily make them the object of conscious reflection. (I called them 'non-conscious'; Freud sometimes calls them 'preconscious'.) But what about those states that cannot 'enter consciousness', or be made the object of conscious reflection so easily? The phenomenon I have in mind is not simply when we make a mistake about some or other of our states of mind—that we would not need to regard as a problem. As I said in Section 1.5, determining the scope of the mental by what is specially accessible does not mean that we must commit ourselves to the infallibility or omniscience of introspection over this realm—just as we need not commit ourselves to the infallibility or omniscience of observation about observable properties. What I have in mind is more serious than a simple mistake: it is when some mental state is so deeply buried in the depths of our mind that reflection cannot access it.

Let me illustrate this with an example chosen from Tolstoy's *Anna Karenina*. Anna, who is married with a child and lives in St Petersburg, visits her brother in Moscow, and there he meets a young officer called Vronski. Vronski and Anna immediately, irrevocably, and fatefully fall in love. Vronski seizes the passion and throws himself at Anna's feet, but Anna, having a husband and a child, is unable to face the reality of her feelings. Not for long though:

At first Anna sincerely believed that she was displeased with him for daring to pursue her. Soon after her return from Moscow, on arriving at a soirée where she had expected to meet him, and not finding him there, she realized distinctly from the rush of disappointment that she had been deceiving herself, and that this pursuit was not merely not distasteful to her, but that it made the whole interest of her life. (Tolstoy 1873–7: pt. II, ch. iv)

Usually, we learn about our own feelings and mental states by reflecting on them; and learn about those of others by relying on what they say and what they do. But Anna's condition with respect to her feelings for Vronski is different. In the first instance, she believes she is displeased with Vronski's repeated declarations of love. That Tolstoy says her belief was 'sincere' emphasizes the extent of her illusion; for, as we see from the next sentence, she was, of course, deceiving herself, yet the deception was so perfect that she could—almost—sincerely believe in it. The way she finally learns about her true feelings is not unlike the way we learn about the feelings of others: by the reaction to a certain situation. If others watched the disappointment on Anna's face after looking around and not finding Vronski, they could learn she was expecting him, and watching her on occasions when Vronski was there, they would not be slow in finding the reason. The important point about Anna's case is not that she did not know about her feelings, or that she was mistaken about them; we have already acknowledged that introspection, like all our cognitive abilities, is fallible. What is important is the way she finally learns the truth: through an inference from one of her feelings.

Anna's predicament is utterly familiar. Probably not in such tragic dimensions, but it is something that we experience about ourselves and about others all the time. As we know from psychological literature, in some cases retrieving repressed feelings or other mental features could be much more difficult than in Anna's case, and may require serious professional help from others. These cases seem to be straightforward counter-examples to the claim that we know our mind in a way no one else does. The truth is that we are often hopelessly ignorant about our feelings, desires, motives, and preferences; that others may know some of these states much better than we do; and that, when we do learn about them, we learn them in the way others would: through inference from our behaviour.

I use the term 'unconscious' to denote these aspects of our mental life, and I will not deny these phenomena. Instead, to defend the Cartesian conception, I shall argue that our understanding of the unconscious is parasitic on our understanding of mental states that are available to conscious reflection. In this, I shall loosely follow an argument that Freud has given for the existence of unconscious mental states, based on the reconciliation of laws of conscious thought and motivation with seemingly anomalous cases.[1]

The starting point of this argument is the observation that 'the data of consciousness have a very large number of gaps in them' (Freud 1915: 168). That is, our actions or series of conscious events sometimes resist common-sense psychological explanations. It is perhaps rarer to observe this in ourselves, but we can certainly observe it in others. So there might be cases where we have absolutely no reason to doubt the sincerity of someone recounting her beliefs, motives, and desires, and yet we cannot make sense of her actions in the light of these using our common-sense psychological explanations. In our particular example, Anna Karenina would sincerely tell you that she has no interest in meeting Vronski, that she finds his pursuit a nuisance, that she sees no reason to change her social habits; yet she would start to frequent society she had not visited before, she would always find herself talking to Vronski on these occasions, and so on. These actions do not make sense, given her avowed feelings.

Freud recounts three options for explaining discrepancies like this. First, we could simply accept the fact that some actions have no explanation. This, however, would go against the whole outlook of science, and its ambition to find intelligible ways for accounting for everything, and Freud thinks this would be unacceptable.

[1] I first learnt about Freud's argument from a very informative essay by Neil Manson (2000). What follows owes a lot to Manson's discussion.

The second option is to offer explanation in non-mental, that is, physiological terms. Some irregular occurrence in Anna's neural paths could cause her to perform the unexpected actions, and we would search for an explanation in terms of her mental states in vain. However, Freud is sceptical about the systematic possibility of providing such accounts. In the light of difficulties with identifying highly specific mental event types with particular brain event types, the scepticism is probably justified. Perhaps one decision to go to a soirée may be explained by a particular chance occurrence in Anna's brain; but, where a systematic pattern of action emerges, it is hard to see how a corresponding physiological regularity would explain Anna's changed social habits.

Even supposing that there is such a physiologically identifiable type, its discovery is surely a long way off—even now, a hundred years after Freud wrote about these issues. But in the meantime we can make sense of cases like Anna's if we retain our normal psychological laws, and choose the third option Freud mentions: positing *unconscious mental states*. Anna's actions would exactly suit a mental state of being infatuated with Vronski and a desire to see him as much as she can. We can, therefore, make sense of her actions if we posit that she possesses such a state unconsciously. And this is indeed Freud's argument for putting forward the existence of unconscious mental states: that, with them, we can explain human actions while upholding the general laws of psychological explanation.

But, and this is the crucial point I would like to add, our *initial* idea of a mental state that has a certain role in governing behaviour is derived from the cases where the state *is* accessible to reflection. If we were not familiar with the paradigmatic cases when a desire, an emotion, an ambition, or a preference guides our actions, and is also available as an object of reflection, then we could not posit their unconscious versions to explain the gaps in consciousness. The demon test delivers the *types* we put on the list of mental features: beliefs, intentions, perceptions, feelings, and so on. When we posit unconscious mental states, we do not add further types to the list; we merely posit unconscious versions of some of the types already on the list.

The claim that 'what belongs to the mind is what is knowable in a special way' is actually ambiguous. It could mean, first, an instruction about how to classify the kind of things we do, or the kind of states we are in, into the mental and the non-mental. The instruction goes as follows: take a certain type of activity, or event, or state, and ask whether it would be possible to do, or undergo, or have it, without ever being in a position to know it in a special way? If the answer is yes, it does not belong to the mind. However, if we find that, in its paradigmatic instances, it can be known in a special way, then it does belong to the mind. So, for example, digestion or the circulation of blood or the breaking-down of toxins by my liver are not mental processes, because they take place and achieve their characteristic effects without my ever having special access to them. But desiring something is a mental state, because desires could not be what they are if they were never available to reflection.

The other sense of delineating what belongs to the mind is to determine which *particular* mental states I am in or which mental events I undergo at a certain time. Thus after I have put together the list and established that beliefs and desires are mental states, I could ask myself which particular beliefs and desires *I have* at the moment. Many of them I can reach by reflection, but others I cannot. So, if the thesis is understood as an instruction to find out *what* I feel, believe, or desire, then it does not work.

But, even in this sense, the idea that the mind is accessible to reflection has a special significance. 'Know thyself' is a hackneyed phrase to be sure, but it is worn out for good reason. We regard actions motivated by unconscious mental states as somehow not in order; a person who lives in ignorance or deception about her real motives or desires is not an autonomous person. We assume that people should strive to make their mind as clear for themselves as possible. We do accept extenuating circumstances for failures of such efforts; if someone's mental balance depends on shutting out some truths about herself, we understand. But that is simply an admission of our less-than-perfect nature, and does not destroy the idea of perfection. Even if it turns out that the Cartesian conception does not describe the actual nature of our minds, what it does is of ultimate importance: it sets an ideal. The Cartesian Mind as an Ideal is, I think, fundamental for our understanding ourselves as persons.

3

PERSONS AND MINDS

3.1 The Importance of the Cartesian List

The application of the demon test results in a list of mental features, and this is the same as our list of what belongs to the mind. That is, what we—including the many critics of the Cartesian conception—study today in the philosophy of mind concerns precisely the phenomena that Descartes classifies as varieties of 'thought': perceptual experiences, sensations, emotions, beliefs, desires, intentions, the will, and so on. In contrast, questions about digestion, metabolism, the growth of our hair or fingernails, running, or sexual reproduction—items on the Aristotelian list that Descartes discards—are outside these concerns. Now is this not just proof of Rorty's claim—that what disguises itself as an intuition about what belongs to the mental—is in fact an uncritical reliance on the Cartesian tradition? So be it, but I see no need for the tone of disapproval. I prefer to say that we owe our conception of the mind to some of Descartes's fundamental insights.

Indeed, we should ask ourselves how easy it would be to get rid of this conception, in favour of, say, an Aristotelian theory, as it has been suggested by some philosophers in the general surge of anti-Cartesianism.[1] Prima facie, there are two ways of drawing

[1] For example, among the contributors to a collection of essays on Aristotle's *De Anima* (Nussbaum and Rorty 1992): including Martha Nussbaum and Hilary Putnam, who were the first to argue that Aristotle is a precursor of modern functionalism; Kathleen Wilkes, who, in a paper entitled '*Psuché* versus the Mind', maintains that Aristotle's notion of the soul is theoretically superior to the Cartesian notion of the mind (ibid. 109–27); or Charles

up a list of phenomena to be studied in the philosophy of mind in an Aristotelian spirit. First, we could take all the faculties of the soul, and include digestion, bodily growth, and movement as psychological phenomena along with the rest. Alternatively, we could limit our attention to the part of the soul that, according to Aristotle, uniquely belongs to human beings—that is, the intellectual soul—and leave out perceptions, emotions, and sensations, since these belong to the sensory part. Thus we could either say that the mind is the soul, the *psyche*, or we could say it is the intellectual part, the *noûs* (and, indeed, some commentators, e.g., Lear 1988 or Shields 2005, render *noûs* as 'mind').

Then consider the following possibilities: for example, David Armstrong's *A Materialist Theory of the Mind* (1968) should either have included a few extra chapters on eating and sex, or should have omitted the chapters on perception and bodily sensations as irrelevant to the topic. If someone finds it hard to countenance this idea, then perhaps she should think twice before urging an opposition to the Cartesian legacy in favour of an Aristotelian conception. (Admittedly quoted somewhat out of context, but would we not find the following statement by Aristotle more congenial to a restaurateur than to a philosopher of mind: 'Since nothing except what is alive can be fed, what is fed is the besouled body and just because it has soul in it. Hence food is essentially related to what has soul in it' (*DA* $416^{b}10$).)

It may be suggested that a list, drawn up in an Aristotelian spirit, should leave out the vegetative part, but include all the faculties belonging to the sensory as well as to the intellectual part of the soul, since the faculties found here, with the exception of movement, are the same as today's psychological phenomena. This could be backed up by the thought that, although we recognize three orders in the realm of living beings—plants, animals, and human beings—our relation to the other two orders is not the

H. Kahn, who claims that Aristotle's real advantage is 'to be exempt from the Cartesian curse of the mind–body opposition with all the baffling paradoxes and philosophical blind alleys that this antithesis gives rise to' ('Aristotle on Thinking', ibid., 359).

same: we are certain kinds of animals, but we are not certain kinds of plants. This suggestion deserves attention; we should avoid ending up with an understanding of Aristotle that places his conception completely outside our present-day concerns with the soul or with the mind.

However, the proposal does leave a few things unexplained. First, the grouping does not emerge as naturally from the Aristotelian theory as the others: we cannot put a third name next to *psyche* and *noûs* that includes only the sensory and the intellectual part. Further, we still need an explanation of why movement should be left out. In fact, there are other faculties that belong to the sensory part according to Aristotle, but do not figure on the Cartesian list of mental phenomena. Such faculties are to be expected to exist in so far as animal life involves functions that plants lack, but that do not, in our present conception, belong to the mind. An example is respiration, which is clearly a function of a living animal, and yet it is not a mental function. To leave out movement and respiration from the list of faculties associated with the sensory part seems ad hoc.

In contrast, there is no need to fiddle with Descartes's list: it is the same as our list of mental phenomena. We saw that we can extricate a systematic method from the Second Meditation to establish what belongs to the mind and what does not; we do not have to rely on some unreflected intuitions, or merely follow scholarly custom. We can contrast this method with Aristotle's principle for putting together his list, which is based on recording the faculties of different orders of living beings. What recommends Descartes's procedure is its result, which is congenial to our present conception.

I admit that my evidence for our conception of what mental phenomena are, taken from contemporary books on the philosophy of mind, can be regarded as somewhat parochial. Rorty's charge that our compartmentalization of human activities into mental and non-mental features has no relevance outside the administrative concerns of the profession should be met. Surely there is more at stake here than what should and should not be included in an anthology on the philosophy of mind, or which topic does or does not deserve a section at a conference on the philosophy of mind. So we need to address the question: why does it matter which features we include on our list of mental phenomena?

3.2 Citizen of Two Worlds

Descartes held that mind and body are different substances that are capable of independent existence. Substance dualism may be criticized for a number of reasons. The very idea of an immaterial substance is hard to square with the prevalent contemporary scientific outlook. A more specific problem arises from the difficulties in understanding how causal interaction is possible between the two different substances (see Lewis 1966; Crane 1995).

Substance dualism is not part of the Cartesian conception of the mind I defend; the classification involved in the demon test does not entail that the mental and the physical belong to different substances. As we know, Descartes believed that his findings in the Second Meditation—his thesis that he is a thinking thing—will eventually lead to the proof that mind and body are different substances. In the Second Meditation, however, he famously expresses some caution about this conclusion. Though he says that the considerations about the demon show that he is not the structure called the human body, nor he is the same as the soul, understood as 'some thin vapour which permeates the limbs', but only a thinking thing, the following possibility still seems viable: 'And yet may it not perhaps be the case that these very things which I am supposing to be nothing, because they are unknown to me, are in reality identical with the "I" of which I am aware? I do not know, and for the moment I shall not argue the point ...' (CSM ii. 18; AT vii. 27). This is where I myself wish to stop. I do not think Descartes's own attempt to prove dualism is successful, but 'I shall not argue the point'. I choose to stay neutral on the question of physicalism versus anti-physicalism.

But, even if we refuse to make substance dualism part of our theory, there is a somewhat more elusive worry, which is not dispelled by this move: that the Cartesian conception offers us a picture of a hopelessly divided human being. The objection would be that, though I do not claim that mind and body are different substances, still I am imposing a partition on the characteristic activities of human beings, seeing them as essentially belonging to two different realms. With a sufficiently hostile rhetoric, one can make this aspect of the Cartesian conception extremely unattractive.

But I believe that, understood appropriately, the claim that our activities belong to two different realms is in fact a fundamental truth about us. The thought has been formulated in countless versions throughout our philosophical and literary tradition. Witness Alexander Pope's famous lines about mankind:

> Placed on this isthmus of a middle state,
> A being darkly wise, and rudely great:
> With too much knowledge for the sceptic side,
> With too much weakness for the stoic's pride,
> He hangs between; in doubt to act or rest,
> In doubt to deem himself a god, or beast...
>
> (*An Essay on Man*, Epistle 2)

Man is a citizen of two worlds. One of the worlds is usually conceived as the world of nature; in some sense, we are like the rest of the universe, subject to its laws, just as stones or trees or animals are. But we are also different—there is a certain aspect of human existence that sets us apart from the rest of the world.

Let me cite a few, somewhat random, examples of our dual nature playing an important role in philosophical theories. Aristotle's definition of human beings as 'rational animals' reflects the same point: on the one hand, man belongs to the animal order of living beings; on the other, his intellect provides a distinctively human aspect—something that possibly relates man to the gods. John McDowell is one of the most forceful contemporary critics of the Cartesian conception of the mind; yet he adopts the thought from Wilfrid Sellars (another influential anti-Cartesian) that the activities of human beings should be characterized as belonging both to the *space of reasons* and to the *space of nature* (see Sellars 1956; McDowell 1994). McDowell is a non-reductive physicalist, so perhaps his upholding some sort of duality about our nature is not all that surprising. But we might expect an eliminative materialist like Richard Rorty to shun the idea of dualism entirely. Not so. Even though according to his theory human beings do not differ in nature from the rest of the material world, he thinks there is an important question for us to answer about why we regard certain creatures—notably other human beings—as being *some of us*; beings who incite certain attitudes, reactions, or treatment from us, and, as such, enjoy a special status compared to the rest of the natural world.

Is this distinctively human characteristic something that is associated with our biological species? Prima facie, the answer is no (though further complications will be noted below). At least at a first glance, we cannot exclude the possibility that other creatures—extraterrestrials, other animals, machines, angels—might share this mode of existence. Therefore it will be a good idea to use a more species-neutral term for this distinctively human way of existence: *personhood*. Human beings are persons, and, to our knowledge, or according to our present conception, they are the only ones we have encountered so far.

3.3 Questions About Persons

Various questions can be raised about personhood, or about the distinctive feature of human existence; I can think of at least four different types. Persons enjoy (or, as the case may be, suffer) special treatment by other persons, and the first question is about what this treatment should precisely be. Persons are held responsible for their actions, and therefore may be subject to resentment or gratitude, reward or punishment. The actions of persons can be judged by moral categories. Further, destroying persons is morally wrong, though this attitude extends further than the group of persons, at least in two notable cases. First, we think human life is to be valued even if it does not sustain the existence of a person yet, or any more (in the sense of personhood relevant, for example, for moral responsibility). Further, it may be argued that destroying great works of art is morally wrong. I suspect, however, that these latter cases ultimately relate to the concern of persons.

The second question is this: what sort of characteristics qualify a creature to be regarded as a person? When searching for the criteria of personhood, we are searching, in Harry Frankfurt's words, for criteria that 'are designed to capture those attributes which are the subject of our most humane concern with ourselves and the source of what we regard as most important and most problematical in our lives' (Frankfurt 1971: 6). Many different answers have been suggested to this question. Frankfurt himself argues that personhood is connected to the structure of our will: that persons alone have the capacity of reflective self-evaluation of their desires. Other—not necessarily incompatible—suggestions include rationality, the capability of autonomous action, the ability to reciprocate, to be self-conscious, to be able to form a life plan, the ability to communicate, and so on (see, e.g., Dennett 1976; Amelie Rorty 1988).

A third question concerns the ontological category to which the only known examples of persons, that is we, belong. This question is often phrased also as a question about the Self, or simply about Us. Answers—many of which are, in this case, incompatible—may include the claim that we are individual substances, psychological (Lowe 1996) or immaterial (Descartes); that we are individual substances belonging to a characteristic secondary substance (Aristotle; Wiggins 2001); that we are a certain kind of animal (Snowdon 1990); that we are our brains (Nagel 1986); that we are certain kind of machines (La Mettrie 1748); that we are bundles of mental events (Hume 1739–40; Parfit 1984); that we are an abstract computer program realized in a certain organism (Putnam 1967) and so on.

A fourth question extensively discussed in philosophy is about personal identity: what are the conditions for someone to remain the same person through time? The answer to this question will probably have connections to answers to the second and third questions.

My interest here is limited mainly to the second question: criteria of personhood. I shall be satisfied with the sketch of answers already given to the first question, and assume accordingly that persons are bearers of moral responsibility and the rightful recipients of the ensuing attitudes. I wish to remain largely non-committal on the details of the third and the fourth questions; I shall come back to these questions briefly in Section 3.5.

The point I have been urging in the previous section was that, no matter how far one departs from the Cartesian conception of human beings, an element of dualism remains in the idea that humankind shares part of its nature with the rest of the natural world, but also possesses something distinctively human. The distinctively human aspect of existence I propose to call personhood. To this I now add a further observation: most or all proposed criteria of personhood are tied (directly or indirectly, as we shall see in Section 3.5) to the possession of some mental feature.

The following quotations by Locke offer a characteristic formulation of the idea that a person is the bearer of moral responsibility, and that only someone in possession of certain kinds of mental features can be regarded as a person:

> we must consider what person stands for;—which, I think, is a thinking intelligent being, that has reason and reflection, and can consider itself as itself, the same thinking thing, in different times and places; which it does only by that consciousness which is inseparable from thinking, and, as it seems to me, essential to it. (1690: II.27.9)

> Person, as I take it, is the name for this self. Wherever a man finds what he calls himself, there, I think, another may say is the same person. It is a forensic term, appropriating actions and their merit; and so belongs only to intelligent agents, capable of a law, and happiness, and misery. (1690: II.27.26)

3.4 Criteria of Personhood

Now *which* psychological attributes are essential for personhood? The answer to this question has probably changed significantly in our intellectual and literary tradition. Which attribute is emphasized depends, among other things, on what the contrast class is—that is, compared to which creatures we consider ourselves as distinctive. One significant demarcation has been between us and the (other) animals: so one question is what distinguishes us from the brutes. Aristotle, and the medieval Scholastic tradition following him, had a very clear answer to this question: it is the possession of the intellect—the intellect, which is capable of grasping universals. The popular definition of a 'person' was that given by Boethius: 'an individual substance of a rational nature'. The distinctively human aspect of existence was the capacity of theoretical and practical reasoning.

Descartes would probably agree with this. Yet various elements of his theory eventually force him to depart from this view, or at least open the way for departure in the subsequent tradition. Descartes retains quite a significant part of the Aristotelian–Scholastic legacy in his conviction that the functions of the sensory part are intimately connected to some bodily activity, and that the rational or intellectual functions are a completely different affair. For when Descartes considers intellectual functions, he is utterly nonplussed as to how these could possibly be realized by matter (see, for example, the Fifth Discourse, CSM i. 140; AT vi. 57 ff.). So, to account for the intellect, the introduction of the immaterial part becomes necessary. But the fact that the intellect interacts with emotions and sensations creates the need for immaterial mental counterparts of the physiological aspects of sensory functions, and hence we get the familiar Cartesian list of mental features. We may wonder what Descartes's reaction would be to contemporary theories of cognitive science explaining intellectual functions, for example, in computational terms, and thereby showing how it may be possible to create intelligence in a purely material being. Perhaps if Descartes had had the chance to read Jerry Fodor, he would have thought twice about dualism.[2]

The idea that the distinctively human aspect of existence is to be found in the use of the intellect—which sets us apart from animals—although still important, has undergone significant change since Descartes's time. One factor in this change was probably the development and widespread acceptance of evolutionary theories, which turned the boundary between animals and humans contingent and historically situated. Another factor must have been the development of artificial intelligence and cognitive science. Now we have machines that are capable of solving tasks that for Aristotle or Descartes, used to be associated exclusively with the human intellect (see also Matthews 1977).

Descartes's departure from Aristotle in separating mindedness and life, and then our departure from Descartes in thinking that matter can accommodate intellect, create another contrast class, from which we have to demarcate ourselves: machines. Actually, we should say *mere* machines, since the possibility that machines can be persons is not to be excluded. We should in fact ask *which* machines we could regard as persons—just as there is the parallel question of which animals, or other biological species in general, we could regard as persons. When demarcation from mere machines is the question, the emphasis shifts from the intellect to the emotions; machines may be very intelligent, but, as long as they

[2] John Cottingham (1992) usefully distinguishes among the theological, scientific, and metaphysical reasons for dualism in Descartes's theory. The metaphysical reasons are the well-known considerations mentioned earlier, in Section 3.2, about the conceivability of disembodied existence. The present considerations—the impossibility of accounting for rational processes in material/mechanical terms—provide the main scientific reasons. The reasons seem fairly independent, and it is an interesting, if moot, point to consider, what would have happened if the scientific outlook had contradicted the metaphysical one.

It is worth noting that one of the reasons most frequently brought to support dualism in contemporary philosophy—that the phenomenal character of conscious sensory or emotional experience cannot be explained in merely physical terms—does not seem to be central in Descartes's considerations about dualism.

do not *feel*, they cannot be counted as some of us. Cases of testing our willingness to accept creatures of different orders as some of us are often found in science-fiction movies. Two examples of how having emotions can upgrade machines or artefacts to the rank of personhood are the characters in Ridley Scott's *Blade Runner* and in Steven Spielberg's *AI*. So it turns out that the emotive part—probably together with at least some elements of the sensory part—is also essential for being a person.

I have already mentioned views that consider the structure of the human will, or the nature of human agency as essential characteristics of persons: these features may include having autonomy, self-control, or being in command of the course of one's life. These are certainly not meant to exclude the previously listed essential characteristics—the intellect and the emotions—since, for example, we expect creatures who exercise self-control to make use of their intellect and to control their emotions.

All these suggestions about what should be regarded as essential for personhood have a great deal of plausibility. In fact, my proposal is that we should take all of them on board. Let us say that a person is someone who doubts, understands, affirms, denies, is willing, is unwilling, imagines, has memories, sensory perceptions, emotions, passions, and so on; an 'intelligent agent, capable of a law, and happiness, and misery'—in short, a creature who has the kind of mind we have. Here—I claim—lies the significance of the Cartesian conception of the mind: it offers us a list of mental phenomena that is put together on a principled basis; and it is the possession of more or less this list of mental attributes that is necessary for someone to be regarded as a person. The list includes every type we can discover in ourselves with the help of reflection, including, of course, the ability to reflect itself.

If someone suggests abandoning the Cartesian conception, it should be considered whether the alternative can offer a replacement. For example, on the Aristotelian conception of the soul, the natural demarcation lines between ourselves and the rest of the world are drawn elsewhere, and hence this conception is less congenial to our own notion of the mind, and the concept of a person that goes with it.

This is an issue that goes well beyond the professional concerns of philosophy. Personhood, as we quoted Harry Frankfurt saying, is the subject of our most humane concerns; and it also has its implications for rights and responsibilities. Our practice concerning whom to endow with the rights of persons may not be consistent, and it is uncertain whether it can ever be made so. But questions about, and improvements on, existing practices will have to look at some guidance in our conception of a person. And this conception, for us, I argue, is best understood with reference to the Cartesian theory.

3.5 The Person and the Human Animal

In the previous section, I distinguished various questions we may ask about persons or about ourselves: the questions of how we should treat persons, of the criteria of personhood, of what sort of things we are, and the question of personal identity. As I said, my primary interest lies in the second question, and I do not intend—nor do I have the space—to develop answers to the third and fourth questions. It may be suggested, however, that my analysis of the criteria of personhood—that someone has the kind of mind we do—commits me to a kind of Lockean position about the other issues, and hence opens my account to the objections that were brought against the Lockean position. I do not think this is the case; let me explain why.

Locke's theory in this context is usually discussed as a theory of identity of persons over time. A broadly speaking Lockean view states that one person existing at a time is (numerically) the same as another person existing at another time if there is some *psychological continuity* between the two: for example, they share some beliefs, desires, and so on, and, crucially, the latter has memories of the experiences of the former and acts to fulfil her intentions. This view clearly suits the straightforward version of the criteria of personhood I suggested: that personhood consists in the possession of certain mental features. The picture is that to be a person is to have certain mental features, and to carry on being the same person is to have an appropriately understood continuity of these mental features.[3]

One of the consequences of this picture is that human beings are not persons at certain stages of their lives: embryos do not have mental features, and neither do people who are in a persistent vegetative state, so they are not persons. The terminology can be a bit confusing here, since 'people' is naturally used as the plural of 'person', but 'people' can also be understood as referring to 'human beings'. I would like to distinguish the term 'human being' (plural: 'human beings'), which refers to a member of the biological species *Homo sapiens*, from the term 'person' (plural: 'persons'), which refers to someone who is a subject of our most humane concerns. If a person has to be in possession of certain mental features, then some human beings are not persons.

To see the possible further consequences of this point, we need to address another issue: namely, what am I? I am certainly a person, but am I essentially a person (or *this* person)? I am also certainly a human being, but am I essentially a human being (or *this* human being)? Different considerations seem to pull in different directions on these issues.

A well-known thought experiment asks us to imagine what would happen if, say, my brain, or part of it, were transplanted to someone else's body, together with my psychological states, while my original body was destroyed. The idea is that, in this case, there would be another human being—in the sense of another human animal, with another body—who would be psychologically continuous with me. There seems to be a powerful intuition that

[3] One of the most influential contemporary defenders of the broadly speaking Lockean view of personal identity is Derek Parfit (1984). Parfit's treatment of the question is complicated by the fact that he does not think that survival requires identity, and he thinks that survival is the one that matters. I am going to ignore this aspect of the debate, because, as far as I see, it does not make any difference to issues of personhood.

the resulting creature would be *me*, and this apparently supports the claim that I am essentially a person, combined with the claim that personal identity consists in psychological continuity.

However, it also seems very natural to say that I was once an embryo, and then a small baby, and this points to a different direction. If we hold on to the idea that a person is someone with the requisite psychological attributes, then the fact that once I was an embryo or a small baby shows that I am not essentially a person, because I already existed before I became a person. Personhood is not part of my essence, but it is more like a phase I go through for a certain period of my existence. Then the following question arises: what are the conditions for my continued existence; that is, what are the conditions for some being in the past or in the future to be *me*? This is not strictly speaking a question of *personal* identity, since some of the beings who are identical to me in the past or the future may not be persons; we could call it instead the question of *my* identity. In any case, since the idea that my identity is the identity of some person is under pressure, perhaps the natural alternative is to say that my identity is the identity of the human animal. I am, in fact, essentially a human being—in the sense of the human animal—whose existence started with the existence of the embryo, and whose existence will continue as long as this animal organism is functioning.

Notice that the view that I am essentially a human animal is compatible with the analysis of the conditions of personhood in psychological terms. If to be a person is to have the kind of mind we have, it is still possible for the defender of the animalist theory to say that human beings are persons for the period of their lives when they are in possession of the required mental features. However, some philosophers have expressed dissatisfaction with this conception of personhood. If the conditions of personhood are given in terms of a list of features, then person is a 'nominal kind', as opposed to a real kind: it is not defined in terms of its underlying real nature (see Lowe 1996). Being a person is like being a teacher, a phase that one goes through, but not an 'abiding sort', as Paul

Snowdon (1990) puts it. But, if questions about persons are indeed connected to what is the most important and problematical in our lives, then we might expect personhood to attach more strongly and meaningfully to our existence than simply like a phase that we go through.

Another consideration against the 'phase' conception of personhood is connected to the first of the four questions about persons I listed above: the treatment due to persons. For example, destroying persons is deeply wrong, persons cannot be treated as commodities, persons are not to be used as means to ends, and so on. This treatment extends to human beings who cannot be regarded as persons according to the straightforward application of the psychological criteria: small babies, severely mentally handicapped people, people in a persistent vegetative state.

One way to overcome this difficulty is to say that persons are members of a *natural kind* whose *normal mature members* possess some characteristic features, including having a certain kind of mind. The apparent advantage of this view is that it makes persons a real kind, as opposed to a nominal kind, since it analyses the conditions for personhood in terms of belonging to a natural kind. Another advantage is that, in this view, members of the kind who do not actually possess the requisite psychological features still count as persons, in virtue of belonging to the kind whose other members do have the right kind of psychology. This view can be regarded as a version of the animalist theory mentioned earlier. But, unlike the previous version we considered, it does not regard personhood as a phase that human animals go through, but rather as something that belongs to the essence of the kind.

Despite these apparent advantages, this view also faces certain difficulties. For example, it is not directly obvious how it accounts for the intuitions that psychological continuity may be enough for my survival even if my animal organism ceases to exist. It is also not clear to me that we should exclude the possibility that something other than a member of a natural kind—for example, a machine—could be a person; or that an exceptionally bright member of an otherwise dull kind could be a person. I cannot attempt to resolve these questions here. The point I would like to make is that my intention is to formulate my proposal so that it is compatible with this theory of personhood. For notice that, although, in this view, conditions of personhood are not given straightforwardly as possession of a list of mental features, still there is an essential reference to this list, through the reference to the characteristic features of normal members of the kind. And that is enough for my purposes. I am happy with the conclusion that the Cartesian list of mental features is crucial in determining the criteria of personhood; either because persons have the kind of mind we have, or because persons are members of a species whose normal members have the kind of mind we have.

David Wiggins is one of the defenders of the view that, for personhood as we know it, identity of persons coincides with the identity of human beings (Wiggins 2001: ch. 7). Wiggins considers a possible objection: that someone may suggest that what matters for personhood is that we experience ourselves as subjects of consciousness, and thus what matters for personal identity is continuity in this respect. Wiggins's reply is that, in fact, the human-being theory can incorporate this circumstance—for cognitive faculties are prominent among the activities that specifically characterize our kind. And we take these into account when we track a human being through her life.

I cannot claim that my proposal is compatible with every detail of every theory of personhood. Something like Wiggins's view may differ from my approach if it searches for conditions for personhood, not only among our mental, but also among our bodily features, since the latter are also characteristic of our kind. In this case, the right kind of psychology may still be a necessary, though not sufficient, condition for personhood, so the list of mental features would still play a crucial role in the criteria for personhood. Even so, I would be somewhat reluctant to embrace this idea, since, as I mentioned when introducing the topic of personhood, it seems to me that creatures other than human beings—other species, extraterrestrials, machines—may also be persons and treated as one of us. In any case, what I wanted to point out in this section is that, by tying the criteria of personhood to the possession of the kind of mind we have, I do not mean to exclude animalist theories of personal identity and their underlying theory of personhood.

To sum up: the worry formulated at the beginning of this section was that my view that to be a person is to be the kind of mind we have commits me to a Lockean view of persons, and exposes my theory to the objections the Lockean view faces. In response, I have explained that I do not want to exclude a weaker or more qualified version of my proposal: where personhood is not defined straightforwardly in terms of possessing the requisite mental features, but indirectly, as being a member of a kind whose normal mature members possess the mental features in question. My main point is that the list of mental features has a deep significance for the issue of personhood, but this point is compatible with a variety of theories of personal identity and personhood.

3.6 Conclusion of Part One

The Cartesian theory of mind has received severe criticism in the twentieth and twenty-first centuries. Anthony Kenny (1989: p. vii) said that—like Ryle—he regarded 'the inheritance of Descartes as being the single most substantial obstacle to a correct philosophical understanding of the nature of human mind'. In these first three chapters, I have attempted to do something towards restoring the reputation of the Cartesian conception. I have analysed the method we can extricate from the Second Mediation to draw up the list of mental phenomena, and I have suggested that the mind, for us, includes the kind of things we can get to know in a way no one else can. I have argued that the resulting list is the same as what we intuitively classify as belonging to the mental; and have tried to show the significance of this by arguing that the possession of the same collection of features (by an individual or members of her kind) is necessary for us to regard someone as a person.

Some readers will perhaps object to this theory being called Cartesian, since I have refused to embrace some central tenets of Descartes's theory: I dispense with the quest for certainty, I do not commit myself to a foundationalist epistemology, and I claim to be neutral on the issue of dualism. Still, as I have tried to show in the previous chapters, Descartes is also the originator of the fundamental idea behind the Cartesian theory defended here; and surely, after so much bad press, it is only right to credit him with an insight for once.

There is another reason why I find it appropriate to call the view defended here Cartesian. In the last few decades, so-called 'externalist' theories of the mind—theories that maintain that certain mental features constitutively depend on facts outside the subject—have gained widespread acceptance. Externalism is sometimes hailed as the most fundamental criticism of the Cartesian conception of the mind, but the targets of the externalist critique are often materialist theories. On this way of looking at things, *internalism*—that is, an opposition to externalism—rather than dualism, is the characteristic feature of the Cartesian view. As John McDowell says in the blurb of Gregory McCulloch's ardently externalist book (1995): 'It is a very important insight that we make almost no headway with the problems Descartes left to the philosophy of mind by rejecting his immateralism'—the real cure being, in McDowell's and McCulloch's view, the rejection of internalism. In the second part of the book, I join the internalism/externalism debate. I shall argue that my Cartesian view is essentially internalist, since, once we accept that privileged accessibility is the mark of the mental, we find ourselves in conflict with externalist theories. But this Cartesian view is fundamental to our conception of the mind. Therefore externalism must go.

PART TWO

Internalism and Externalism

4

THE INTERNAL AND THE EXTERNAL

4.1 The Boundary Between the Internal and the External

In the first three chapters, I have argued for a certain 'Cartesian' conception of the mind; according to this conception, the mind is what is known through a faculty that provides us privileged access to its subject matter. At the end of Chapter 3, I said that, even though I depart from Descartes on a number of important points, one reason why I still find it appropriate to call the theory 'Cartesian' is that *internalism* is often regarded as the essential feature of a Cartesian theory, and my own conception is internalist. That is, I believe that a subject's mental features are determined by her internal states. In order to show that my Cartesian theory is indeed internalist, I have to establish a connection between privileged accessibility as the mark of the mental, on the one hand, and the thesis of internalism, on the other. It has been argued before that externalism is incompatible with the thesis of privileged access to our thought contents, but the charge of incompatibility has been also heavily disputed. I believe that progress will be made in this rather complicated debate only if we first clarify what exactly the internalism/externalism controversy is. This is going to occupy us in this chapter.

This chapter draws on material in Farkas (2003) and Farkas (2006). The present discussion (hopefully) answers some objections I had not quite realized before and that emerged from various reactions to the 2003 paper.

Externalism about cognitive content has been discussed for almost forty years, and has become almost an orthodoxy in the philosophy of mind. A number of views have been called 'externalist' even within this area, but I shall focus my attention on what may be called 'Twin Earth externalism', the version of externalism that is expressly motivated by Twin Earth style arguments. The prototype of these arguments is, of course, Putnam's argument in 'The Meaning of "Meaning"' (1975a). The story has been told many times, but in any case I will state it for the record.

We are asked to imagine a planet called 'Twin Earth', which is just like Earth in most respects, with one difference. The transparent, colourless, odourless liquid that flows in the rivers of Twin Earth, and that people on Twin Earth who speak a language that sounds just like English call 'water', is not H_2O, but has a different complex chemical composition, which we shall abbreviate as XYZ. H_2O and XYZ are distinguishable only by using sophisticated chemical analysis, but in normal circumstances they look, smell, and taste the same. Putnam's first contention is that XYZ is not water. If a spaceship travelled from Earth to Twin Earth, travellers from Earth might think first that Twin Earth had water; later, when chemical analysis was done, they would find that they had been wrong. Since XYZ is not water, our word 'water' does not refer to XYZ, and parallel considerations would show that the Twin Earth word 'water' does not refer to H_2O.

Next we are asked to go back in time to say 1750, when the chemical composition of water was not known. Putnam maintains that the word 'water' had the same reference back then as it has now; the subsequent discovery that water is H_2O has not changed the meaning and hence the reference of 'water', but simply taught us something about the stuff we have been calling 'water' all along. If this is right, then already back in 1750 the word 'water' as used on Earth referred only to H_2O, and not to XYZ. And similar considerations about Twin Earth would show that their word 'water' referred only to XYZ, and not to H_2O.

Now enter Oscar, an inhabitant of Earth who lived in 1750, and suppose that, by some cosmic coincidence, there lived someone on Twin Earth, call him 'Twin Oscar' (known to his friends simply as 'Oscar'), who was an exact replica of Oscar, and shared the same history throughout his lifetime. Oscar refers exclusively to H_2O by 'water', and Twin Oscar refers exclusively to XYZ by 'water'. Therefore, the story continues, the belief Oscar expresses by the sentence 'Water quenches thirst' is true if and only if H_2O quenches thirst, while the belief Twin Oscar expresses by the sentence 'Water quenches thirst' is true if and only if XYZ quenches thirst. Since the truth conditions of their beliefs are different, so are the contents of these beliefs. But we agreed that Oscar and Twin Oscar are internally the same. Consequently, the content of some mental states depends on factors outside the individual. This is externalism, which is opposed to the internalist view that the content of our mental states is determined by our internal states. I shall analyse and criticize this argument in Chapter 7, but, before I do that, we first have to find out what exactly externalism involves.

The externalist thesis is formulated in a variety of ways:

- The content of a subject's thoughts depends on, or is individuated by, facts *external* to the subject.
- The content of a subject's thoughts does not supervene on her *internal* states.
- A subject's having certain thoughts presupposes or entails the existence or particular nature of things that are *external* to the subject.
- The content of a subject's thoughts are not determined by her *intrinsic* properties.
- Some content properties are *relational*.

There may be other versions, but all versions agree in one point—namely, drawing a boundary between the external and the internal, or some related notions. Since I shall focus on the internal/external distinction, let me say a few words about the other terms.

The claim that content properties are (determined by) *relational* properties is contrasted to the claim that these properties are *intrinsic*; though some prefer to say that the opposite of 'intrinsic' is 'extrinsic'. The precise definition of 'intrinsic' is by no means a trivial issue, as shown by a considerable debate on this subject—see, for example, the summary in *The Stanford Encyclopedia of Philosophy* (Weatherson 2007). I do not want to get involved in the details of this debate, since hopefully nothing I say depends on them. The basic notion of intrinsic properties is something like this: those properties that depend wholly on the individual itself, and not on the rest of the world. Sometimes this is further explained as the properties that an individual could have even if the rest of the world did not exist. All these notions rely on the distinction between the *individual* and the *rest of the world*. We must then have an idea of what belongs to, or is part of, the individual, and an idea of its 'boundaries', or where the 'rest of the world' starts. This is the same as what we are trying to capture by saying that things are 'internal' or 'external' to an individual, so it seems that it is the latter distinction that we have to clarify first. In the following discussion, while focusing on the internal/external distinction, I shall indicate how my findings apply to the formulations of externalism that rely on the intrinsic/non-intrinsic distinction.

In order to understand the exact content of the externalist thesis, we need to understand what the phrases 'internal' and 'external' mean. There is one interpretation that seems to be accepted in many discussions: that 'external' means *external to the body or skin (or brain) of the subject* (cf., e.g., Burge 1988: 650; Jackson and Pettit 1988: 220; McCulloch 1995: 189; Boghossian 1997: 163; Davies 1998: 322; MacDonald 1998: 124; McLaughlin and Tye 1998: 285.) Then the externalist thesis claims that the content of a subject's thoughts or sentences depends on facts external to her skin. This conception certainly gets support from Putnam's original formulation, that 'meanings ain't in the head' (Putnam 1975a). However, I shall try to show that the point of externalism is not really about the individuating facts being inside or outside the skin.

As I said, my interest here lies in the version of externalism expressly motivated by Twin Earth style arguments, which feature two subjects whose internal states are stipulated to be the same. This suggests a way of finding out what 'external' and 'internal' mean. We have to focus on the *relation between the Twins*; what is this thing they share, which, according to the externalist, is not sufficient to individuate the content of their thoughts? If we can say what this is, then we have a grasp on what 'internal' is; and everything that the Twins may not share will be 'external'. (There is a connection here with intrinsic properties: for one suggestion is that intrinsic properties are those that duplicates share; so we need to find out in what sense the Twins are duplicates of each other.)[1]

Given the assumption that 'internal' means 'inside the skin' and 'external' means 'outside the skin', the usual strategy has two subjects whose in-the-skin states are (qualitatively) physically identical. So the relation between the Twins is *identity in qualitative physical make-up*. In what follows, I shall argue that the stipulation about identity in physical make-up fails to secure the point of the externalist argument. This means that the interpretation of 'internal' as 'inside the skin' is inadequate; the boundary between the internal and the external should not be drawn around the skin.

4.2 Identity in Physical Make-Up

If internal physical duplicates have different thought contents—as the conclusion of the Twin Earth argument claims—this is bad

[1] The Twin Earth scenarios that stipulate a difference in the physical environment of the Twins support one variety of argument for externalism. Another highly influential version stipulates differences in the Twins' social environment, in particular, in the use of words in their linguistic communities (see the examples about 'elm' and 'beach' in Putnam 1975a, and about 'arthritis' in Burge 1979). The view that the content of one's thought depends on features of one's social environment is sometimes called 'anti-individualism', in which case, I take it that it is a specific form of externalism, for the features of a subject's social environment are decidedly external to the subject. In other cases 'anti-individualism' is used simply as a synonym for 'externalism' (e.g., in Brown 2004). I shall use the term 'internalism' throughout, and regard individualism or social internalism as a variety of internalism, so hopefully my conclusions cover all varieties.

news for all theories that claim that contents supervene on internal physical properties. This argument still fails to address those dualists who deny the supervenience of contents on physical states, arguably with Descartes himself among them. To remedy this problem, and make the externalist argument effective against dualist internalist theories, one could suggest that, in addition to internal physical sameness, we should also stipulate that the Twins should share their *intrinsic non-physical* properties (that is, if they have any). It is not obvious that this move helps; but, however that may be, there is another difficulty.

Arguably, at least some diseases are natural kinds: they have some superficial properties (the symptoms), on the basis of which we normally identify them, and some underlying structure that is responsible for their superficial properties—for example, a certain inflammation caused by some bacteria. We can then design the following Twin Earth case: suppose that the disease known as 'meningitis' on Twin Earth, which has exactly the same symptoms and overall effects as meningitis on Earth, is in fact not caused by the bacterium meningococcus (as on Earth), but by a different bacterium, which we will call 'XYZ'. Consider Oscar on Earth, suffering from meningitis back in 1750, when the bacterium causing meningitis was unknown, and Twin Oscar on Twin Earth, who is as similar to Oscar as possible, except that at the same time he is suffering from the disease caused by XYZ. Then it seems that the argument could proceed in the same way as in the original Twin Earth case: Oscar's thought 'meningitis is a dangerous disease' has a different content from Twin Oscar's parallel thought, because Oscar is thinking about meningitis, and Twin Oscar is thinking about the disease caused by XYZ. We reached a conclusion very similar in spirit to the externalist thesis, but the relevant individuating facts in this case are inside the body.

It may be noticed that the original Twin Earth example involving 'water' is in fact similar to the meningitis case: as it has been repeatedly pointed out, the Twins of the original example cannot be physically identical, since the human body contains a significant amount of water. The objection is usually not regarded as very serious; the general feeling was that we could find a better example, about a substance that is not found in the human body, so everyone continued using the water example. I suggest that our willingness to overlook this problem in the original argument is better explained by the fact that the point of externalism is not whether the individuating facts are inside or outside the body. In fact, this becomes even clearer in a later version of the argument Putnam offers: in that version, Twin Earth water is 20 per cent grain alcohol, and the body chemistry of Twin people is changed so that they react to this mixture as we do to water (Putnam 1981: 23). This argument seems to pass as an argument for Twin Earth externalism, and yet the condition of internal physical sameness is obviously violated. The meningitis example helps to bring out the point even more clearly, since our stereotype about meningitis is formed on the basis of its occurrences in the human body, whereas the same is not true of water.

Some philosophers motivate the externalist analysis of the water argument simply by intuitions, others back up their intuitions with a certain theory of natural kind terms. It seems that, whichever motivation is at work in the original example, it is also present in the meningitis case. So, if any argument for externalism based on natural kind terms is worth anything, the meningitis case is just as good an example as any other natural kind. Or, to put it in another way: if someone claimed that Oscar and Twin Oscar meant something different by 'meningitis' because of the unknown microscopic difference in their bodies, then this would be as unacceptable to someone with internalist inclinations as any other externalist conclusion. If this is right, then we have a perfectly good argument for externalism that is based on the 'external' facts being inside the body.

Notice that here it would not help much if we formulated the conclusion of the Twin Earth argument in terms of the intrinsic/extrinsic distinction, instead of the internal/external. Gabriel Segal, who defines the internalism/externalism controversy in terms of intrinsic and relational properties, gives chemical and micro-structural constitution as examples of intrinsic properties (Segal 2000: 1–2). Susana Nuccetelli formulates the debate in terms of 'local' properties, where 'local' (which she uses as synonymous with 'internal' or 'intrinsic') properties are those that do not presuppose the existence of anything other than the subject, or, equivalently, shared by internal replicas. And her example of an internal property is having kidneys (Nuccetelli 2003: 3). On any theory that holds that my body is (part of) me, facts about bodily constitution are intrinsic properties. So, in the meningitis example, the externalist conclusion is reached by pointing out that the Twins have different thoughts because of their different intrinsic properties. Then 'internal' in the externalist thesis cannot mean 'inside the body', and we should seek for another interpretation. Those who find this convincing may want to skip to the next section; those who do not are perhaps worrying about some of the objections I will try to address in the rest of this section.

It strikes me as obvious that the point of the meningitis argument is exactly the same as the point of the water argument, but some will perhaps disagree. The objection could run like this:

> no one denies that some in-the-skin facts make a difference to the content of our thoughts, therefore it should not come as a surprise that subjects with different physical make-up have different thoughts. The point of the Twin Earth arguments is that *even if* you stipulate molecule for molecule identity, the thoughts could still differ. Given that we have this *stronger* thesis, why should we care about the weaker thesis? Anyway, externalism *is* the view that mental contents do not supervene on bodily states, so the issue between the internalist and the externalist is whether *molecule for molecule identical Twins* can have different thoughts or not. The protagonists of the meningitis example *are not Twins in this sense*, so whatever we say about their thoughts will be irrelevant to the issue of externalism.

Let me offer the following analogy to illustrate what seems to me wrong with this objection. Suppose that we stipulate that our

Twins, Oscar and Twin Oscar, should be molecule for molecule identical, and, furthermore, that they should wear 'identical' ties. Then we run the usual Twin Earth argument, and come up with the following interesting thesis: mental contents do not supervene on bodily states plus tie states. Interesting indeed, someone will say, but could you not run the argument without the ties? Our reply comes readily: if we have the stronger thesis about bodily *plus* tie states, why should we care about the weaker thesis? Anyway, tie externalism *is* about Twins who satisfy the given stipulations; so, whatever you say about Twins who are *merely* molecule for molecule identical, it will be irrelevant to our purposes.

I assume that my opponents will acknowledge that defending tie externalism is pointless, but they may still remain unconvinced that the point I am making here has much significance. They will now admit that the Twins do not have to be molecule for molecule identical: for example, Oscar could be an inch taller than Twin Oscar, and the argument will work just as well. After all, they will say, not even an internalist thinks that *every* aspect of our internal states is relevant for determining the content of our thoughts, though, of course, we cannot tell exactly which ones are relevant and which ones are not. So it is not surprising that we can run Twin Earth arguments with subjects who are not exactly internally identical.

But this reply still fails to address the point raised by the meningitis example. In some cases, internalist and externalist could happily agree that an internal physical difference implies a mental difference between two subjects; for example, in cases where the internal difference concerns some brain state that has an established connection with certain representations. In other cases, they can happily agree that an internal physical difference is unlikely to make any difference to thought contents—for example, if Oscar's appendix is a few millimetres longer than Twin Oscar's appendix. The striking feature of the meningitis case is the *disagreement* between the internalist and the externalist: there is an internal difference, the internalist thinks that there is no reason to think there is a mental difference, and the externalist thinks that there is every reason to think that there is one. Why? Why did this case not invoke the agreement seen in the other cases? It seems that, without answering this question, we cannot really understand what is really at stake in the internalism/externalism debate.

Here is a final worry before I move on. Someone might say that internalists and externalists could all agree about particular cases: for example, if Oscar is an inch taller than Twin Oscar, or if Oscar is a gram heavier than Twin Oscar, this does not change much the essence of the externalist arguments. However, this objector might insist that there is no way to *specify what counts in general* as a relevant difference in bodily states—relevant in the sense that it gives the externalist his point—and what does not. Ties come off easily, but bodily parts do not. Therefore, the argument continues, the only logical or natural way to draw the boundary between external and internal is around the body or the brain. But this objection works only if there is indeed no other way to draw the boundary, and I want to show precisely that there is.

4.3 External/Internal Defined

In the previous section, I noted that internalism can come in both a physicalist and a dualist version, and a general externalist thesis should be effective against dualist versions of internalism as well. Further, I argued that externalism—or something very much like it—can arise with respect to facts inside the body. The next question is whether it is possible to define externalism in a way that accommodates these two points, especially the second. The new definition must depart from the idea that the skin is the boundary between the internal and the external. I admit that this creates a certain difficulty: if the usual understanding is based on the in-the-skin/outside-the-skin conception, then it seems that I simply change the subject if I propose a modification. After all, if numerous philosophers explicitly say—and they do—what they mean by externalism, then we should take their word for it. I do not want to dispute this. Still, I think it is legitimate to ask what further motives may lie behind the externalist thesis, which may be brought to the surface by considering the points about dualism and the meningitis case. I shall try to explain how my proposal overlaps with the usual understanding, and leave to the reader to decide between the usual understanding and my suggestion.

So suppose that at least it makes sense to ask whether some understanding of externalism can accommodate the points raised in the previous section. What we need then is a characterization of a relation between the Twins that (i) establishes an identity or equivalence between the Twins in some respect; (ii) makes the Twins in the meningitis case equivalent in this respect; and (iii) implies 'internal' sameness in a way that is applicable to dualist theories. As I said earlier, the characterization of this relation will deliver the notion of the relevant boundary between the internal and the external; whatever is common to the Twins in this respect is internal to a subject, and the externalist conclusion is that this is what is insufficient to individuate mental content.

One crucial element in the Twin Earth set-up is that H_2O and XYZ are distinguishable only by using sophisticated chemical analysis, but in normal circumstances they look, smell, and taste the same. So, if a spaceship travelled from Earth to Twin Earth, the travellers would first think that they had found water on the other planet. Think about what would spoil the Twin Earth argument. Let's call the liquid composed of XYZ 'twater'. (Of course, people on Twin Earth call the same stuff 'water', just as they call Twin Oscar simply 'Oscar'.) If twater was blue and bitter in ordinary circumstances, an internalist could easily agree that 'water' meant something different on Earth and Twin Earth. Imagine that you now see a glass of water, you taste it, and it quenches your thirst. We know that the situation of Earth and Twin Earth is exactly symmetrical (they call *our* planet Twin Earth). Now, if *this* were Twin Earth with XYZ on it, the situation would be subjectively indistinguishable: the liquid called 'water' would look, smell, and taste the same, and it would quench your thirst just as well. And all your past experiences with twater would have been subjectively the same as your experiences with water. In the versions where the body chemistry varies from Earth to Twin Earth you should imagine a counterfactual swap of body chemistries. This suggests that the relation between the Twins is that *things appear (look, taste, smell, sound) the same for them; or the world is (and has always been) the same from their subjective viewpoint.* The externalist thesis would then be that thought contents could be different even if appearances were the same; that *content depends on factors that are external to the subject's point of view.*

Let me list the reasons that recommend this relation as the basis for formulating the internalism/externalism debate. First, at least prima facie, one way to create subjectively indistinguishable situations is to keep the internal physical make-up of the subject constant, while varying the outside causes of her experiences. Internal physical sameness (with a few extra assumptions) then preserves the subjective viewpoint. This means that all customarily discussed Twin Earth cases, involving identity in physical make-up, would turn out Twin Earth cases on this understanding too, so I can take on board all the examples that are discussed on the traditional understanding.

Secondly, the same notion seems to be working in the brain-in-a-vat scenario. According to the familiar sceptical hypothesis I have already mentioned in Chapter 1, I could be a bodiless brain that is placed in a vat and fed by a perfect global hallucinatory experience through a computer. The crucial point here is that I cannot subjectively distinguish my present situation from the situation of being a vat brain; that is why the hypothesis threatens to undermine our knowledge of the external world. Internalists and (some) externalists disagree about vat brains: the former say that they have the same thoughts as their embodied counterparts, while the latter deny this. My proposal about the content of the externalist thesis fits this situation nicely: my internalist position is that, since everything seems the same for vat-brains, their thought contents are the same; one would have to be an externalist to deny this.

Thirdly, the proposal covers the cases discussed in Section 4.2. In the meningitis case, and in both versions of the water case, the point of the argument is not that the Twins are molecule for molecule identical (as they are not); the crucial stipulation in the scenario is that, things appear the same for the Twins. The proposal is also applicable to dualist theories. The key of the demon hypothesis is that, if we were deceived by the demon, *everything would appear the same.* Descartes believes that, even if this were the case, all our thoughts would be the same—and this makes it immediately clear why Descartes's theory is an internalist theory.

Fourthly, understanding the relation between the Twins in terms of things appearing the same is also applicable to other brands of externalist arguments. Putnam's argument (1975a) from the division of linguistic labour, and Burge's argument (1979) for social externalism, both involve imagining two linguistic communities where the use of certain expressions differ. Then we are to place a Twin in each of these communities, and, according to the argument, they will have different concepts. These arguments would *not* be arguments for externalism if the Twins somehow *registered* the relevant differences in usage. The crucial assumption of the scenario is again that, if the Twins were counterfactually swapped, *the situation would appear the same for the subject.*

In fact, in the literature on externalism, the Twins' situation is characterized in these terms all the time, as the following few examples will illustrate. Jessica Brown (2004: 38) says the counterfactual Twin scenario 'is set up in such a way that things would seem subjectively just the same to the subject if she were in that environment'. Gary Ebbs (2005) describes the Twins' situation as 'subjectively equivalent'. Anthony Brueckner (1990: 449) says that, 'if I were on Twin-Earth thinking that some twater is dripping, things would seem exactly as they now seem (and have seemed)'. Simon Blackburn (1984: 324), defending internalism, describes a series of Twin Earth style scenarios where 'everything is the same from the subject's point of view'. In criticizing Blackburn's internalist position, John McDowell (1986: 157) still agrees as far as 'the uncontentiously legitimate category of things that are the same across the different cases is how things seem to the subject'. (Though McDowell denies that there would be 'something'—a mental state, for example—that is the same across these situations; I shall come back to this question in Section 4.5.) And I could add many more examples to this list.

Tyler Burge is one of the few philosophers who does address the problem of formulating internalism in a way that is applicable to non-materialist theories (see also Pettit 1986: 17–18). Burge's initial suggestion (1986: 117) is that individualism is 'the thesis that a person's phenomenological, qualitative mental phenomena fix all the person's mental states, including those (like thoughts, desires, intentions) with intentionality and representational characteristics'. In other words, the relation between the Twins is sameness of 'phenomenological, qualitative mental phenomena'. This is very similar to my suggestion. Burge, however, worries about this proposal, because it appears to presuppose a questionable distinction between the phenomenological and the intentional. This worry needs to be addressed, as well as the question of what it means exactly that things look the same for two subjects. This will occupy us for the rest of this chapter, as well as for the next.

4.4 Twin Situations

I argued that the internalism/externalism controversy should be formulated with reference to the relation of things appearing the same, or situations being indistinguishable. However, this relation can be understood in different ways. I shall proceed by focusing on certain pairs of situations that intuitively stand in this relation, and then try to see what exactly is common to them.

Here is an example of such a pair. Consider, on the one hand, the actual situation of Oscar on Earth, drinking a glass of transparent, odourless, tasteless liquid he calls 'water'; and consider Oscar in a counterfactual situation, having grown up on Twin Earth, where he is again drinking a glass of transparent, odourless, tasteless liquid he calls 'water'. As usual, we assume that in Oscar's counterfactual life on Twin Earth everything is the same as in his actual life, apart from the chemical composition of the stuff called 'water'. The crucial feature of these situations is that, in some sense, they are *subjectively indistinguishable*.

The Twin Earth thought experiment is often told, not as the story of one person in an actual and counterfactual situation, but as the story of two people in the same world: Oscar on Earth, and his Doppelgänger, Twin Oscar on Twin Earth. It seems that there is an interesting relation between Oscar's water-drinking experience and Twin Oscar's twater-drinking experience too, which does not hold between say Oscar's water-drinking experience and Twin Oscar's *wine*-drinking experience: namely that the water- and twater-drinking experiences involve things seeming the same.

Another important group of examples is familiar from discussions in epistemology, or scepticism, or the theory of perception. The issue is often introduced in something like the following fashion:

> Suppose I now see a teacup in front of me. Would it not be possible that everything seems the same, and yet the teacup I take myself to be perceiving is not there? Would it not be possible to have a hallucination that was subjectively indistinguishable from my present experience? If this is a genuine possibility, how do I know it is not happening right now?

The fact that such hallucinations are possible is supposed to be highly significant for the understanding of perception and perceptual knowledge. Central to these considerations is the idea of a veridical perception and the 'corresponding' hallucination—that is, the hallucination that I am wondering whether I am having instead of my perception. The brain-in-a-vat example I mentioned briefly in Chapter 1 is an extension of this idea: Oscar's vat-brain counterpart has hallucinations corresponding to each of Oscar's veridical perceptions. These experiences, just like the water- and twater-drinking experiences, are subjectively indistinguishable.

I shall call all these pairs of situations 'Twin situations'; Twin situations can involve two actual subjects in different environments—Earth and Twin Earth, or embodied and vat-world—or an actual and a counterfactual subject in different environments. The reason I consider all these pairings is that an internalist would be committed to the claim that contents (and all other mental features) can remain the same through all these variations. In the traditional understanding, this is a result of the fact that a subject could have actual or counterfactual, Twin Earth, hallucinating, or vat-brain counterparts who have the same internal physical make-up. In the alternative understanding that I recommend, it should still be the case that 'internal sameness' can remain constant throughout these external variations. I am thereby making the claim that the *same relation* is constitutive of all the different types of Twin situations; that, for example, the relation between the experiences of Oscar and his *Twin Earth* counterpart is the same as the relation between a veridical perception and a corresponding hallucination, and hence between the experiences of Oscar and his *vat-brain* counterpart. This claim can be challenged. So it is part of my task to show that there *is* a relation that covers all types of Twin situations—again, because I take this to be part of the internalist commitment.

The question is: how should we understand the relation constitutive of the Twin situations? This is important, first, because this relation is the basis of the internalism/externalism controversy. Internalists say that subjects in the Twin situations have the same mental features; externalists deny this. But, quite apart from the role it may play in defining the internalism/externalism controversy, this is a question that certainly deserves our attention. In each type of case, there does seem to be an interesting relation between Twin situations, something that every theory of experience should account for.

4.5 Physical or Functional Equivalence

First, let me point out again that there is little hope that we can give an illuminating analysis of the Twin situations in purely physical terms. This is shown by the examples considered so far, like the meningitis case or indeed the water case itself. In general, it is very plausible that two experiences could be indistinguishable even if their physical realizations were somewhat different; all we need to support this idea is any possibility of multiple physical realization for experiences. On certain views, internal physical sameness of Twins would be sufficient for creating indistinguishable situations; but I doubt that the condition would be necessary on any theory. So we cannot simply equate the relation between the Twins with physical sameness.

It may be suggested that the relation constitutive of Twin situations could be understood in terms of behavioural or functional sameness: this would be less strict than complete qualitative identity in physical make-up, but could perhaps capture what is shared by the Twins. The idea is that Oscar's behaviour vis-à-vis water is the same as Twin Oscar's behaviour vis-à-vis twater. The behavioural or functional specification would be formulated in non-mental terms, and restricted to narrow states—that is, it would take into account only the subject's bodily states. We need the latter constraint because, if we allowed descriptions of the Twins' behaviour in terms of relations to their environment, their behaviour might turn out to be different: one is holding a glass of *water*, the other is holding a glass of *twater*. Still, a lot of people had the feeling that, in some sense, Oscar's and Twin Oscar's behaviour is the same, though this sameness is more difficult to characterize than one would initially think—precisely because the most natural way to describe behaviour is with reference to the environment, and the environments in this case could be different in all sorts of way.

But, even if we do succeed in finding such a description, there is reason to think that behavioural or functional equivalence in itself cannot capture what it is for two experiences to be subjectively indistinguishable or to seem the same. Behavioural or functional sameness does not guarantee that both subjects are conscious, and hence that they have experiences in the first place. One of them could be a functionally equivalent zombie: in that case, we could hardly say that everything seems the same to them. Notice that this possibility is consistent with physicalism, even in a necessarily supervenient version; we have allowed that the two subjects could be physically different, so perhaps one of them is missing the bit that is needed for being conscious, while being functionally equivalent to the other.

These considerations suggest that a characterization in merely physical terms will not capture the relation between the Twins; instead, I suggest, we should look for an analysis in mental terms. I see two basic directions to develop such an analysis. The first we may call a *metaphysical* direction, in the sense that the account would be based on the *sameness of certain mental properties* between the two situations. The other direction is what I call *epistemic*, which would be based on some epistemic attitude a subject has towards Twin situations. The next section considers the first option, which is the one I am going to adopt.

4.6 Phenomenal Properties Introduced

Let me start my own account of the Twin situations with the claim that perceptual experiences have a *phenomenal character*, which determines what it is like to have that experience. I also claim that the phenomenal character of the Twins' experiences is the same. This is how I suggest developing this notion. An ordinary perceptual experience is a mental event; an event of something appearing (looking, sounding, smelling, tasting, feeling) to us in a certain way; or of it appearing to us that something is in a certain way (this description is more suitable for hallucinations, where there is not literally any 'thing' that appears to us in some way). The mental nature of the experience is given by how things appear to us when having that experience. In the case of perceptual experiences, this is the experience's phenomenal character, or what it is like to have that experience.

We can extend this treatment to *sensations*. A sensation is the same as things feeling in a certain way; and, in so far as two sensations involve feeling in the same way in some respect—for example, two sensations both involve that I feel warmed—the same feeling is involved in both, and hence they share a phenomenal property. When I say that 'things' feel a certain way, I do not necessarily mean that the sensation has an *object*. I have in mind constructions to characterize a sensation like 'how does it feel being up there?' or 'it feels cold around here', where the 'it' fulfils a function similar to the 'it' of 'it is raining', and hence does not denote a particular *thing* feeling cold, unless of course that thing is the subject herself. It may turn out on further analysis that some, or all, sensations have an intentional object—perhaps the subject herself or part of the subject—but I would like the initial characterization to remain neutral on this question.

If two experiences involve things appearing or feeling in the same way in a certain respect, then, to that extent, their phenomenal character is shared. If this book on the table appears blue and rectangular shaped to me, and, when I turn my eyes to the bookshelf, this other book appears to have the same colour and shape, then the phenomenal character of these two experiences shares some properties: the same apparent colour and shape are involved in both. When I characterize a visual experience as 'the book appearing blue', I mean that this *is* the experience, not that this is the content of the experience. The content of the experience is that the book *is* blue, not that it appears blue. The fact that it appears in this way to me is the same as the fact that I have a certain visual experience.

When I say that things appear the same (colour, shape, or otherwise), this amounts to saying that the experiences of things looking in this way for some subjects have a common phenomenal property. So appearance properties are primarily properties of *experiences*; when we talk of, say, the book having an appearance property, this should be understood as derivative of the property that an experience of that book has. If we say that white things appear red in red light, this is to be understood as a reference to the typical experiences of certain kind of perceivers in those circumstances.

A further class of mental events with an obvious phenomenal or what-it-is-like character are occurrent emotions. And, in fact, we can further extend the notion of phenomenal character to *all conscious thought*. Sensory experiences and certain kinds of emotions are usually offered as the paradigmatic examples of conscious mental states or events with a 'what-is-it-like' character; but several philosophers have argued that the notion makes very good sense applied to pure conscious thought. Galen Strawson (1994) convincingly showed that there is a phenomenology of understanding that is present in cognitive processes and cannot be identified with the sensory aspects of experience. Terence Horgan, John Tienson, and George Graham (Horgan and Tienson 2002; Horgan et al. 2004) have presented a whole range of mental features of our conscious life that have their distinctive phenomenology. These include 'the *phenomenology of agency*: the what-it's-like of apparently *voluntarily controlling*'; the '*conative and cognitive* phenomenology: the what-it's-like of consciously (as opposed to unconsciously) undergoing various occurrent propositional attitudes', which further include '(i) the phenomenology of *attitude type* and (ii) the phenomenology of *content*' (Horgan et al. 2004: 305; see also Siewert 1998; Loar 2003). What it is like to think about water is different from what it is like to think about wine: the difference is something that impinges on one's consciousness. Wanting to drink wine or firmly deciding to refrain from drinking wine are again mental features that are phenomenologically very different. The arguments for this extended sense of the phenomenal are often based on invitations to reflect upon the nature of conscious experience. David Pitt (2004) puts forward a different argument, which is very congenial to the project of this book. Pitt argues that the possibility of introspective knowledge of contents shows that cognition must have a phenomenology.

As Horgan and Tienson (2002: 522) remark, 'the overall phenomenology of these kinds of intentional states involves abstractable aspects which themselves are distinctively phenomenological'. This is the key to establishing sameness of phenomenal properties of, say, cognitive attitudes in a way similar to sameness of phenomenal properties of experiences. Wanting to drink wine and not wanting to drink wine share the abstractable phenomenology of thinking about wine; wanting to drink wine and wanting to drink water share the abstractable phenomenology of wanting. The hope is that the entire range of our conscious mental events, everything that passes in the stream of consciousness, can be characterized with the help of phenomenal properties.

My suggestion is to characterize the relation between Twins as the sameness of the phenomenal character of all their conscious thought and experience. So when we say that everything seems the same for the Twins, we say that there is a way things seem for them, which is the same. The suggestion builds on the extended sense of 'phenomenal' properties I explained above, with phenomenology attributed to cognition, as well as to sensory or emotive features. If my arguments in this chapter and the next are correct, and this is indeed the best way to characterize the Twin situations, then we may have, in this account, an additional argument for the extended sense of the phenomenal. The Twins should have phenomenally identical sensory experiences of the liquid known to them as 'water', but their cognitive attitudes towards this liquid should also be the same, in some sense. The suggestion is that this sense is the sameness of the phenomenology of cognition.

4.7 Narrow Content

The suggestion to characterize the relation between Twins as the sameness of the phenomenal character of all their conscious thought and experience is one of the 'metaphysical' accounts of the relation constitutive of the Twin situations. If we wanted to capture the relation between the Twins in terms of shared mental properties, an alternative (or additional) option would be to say that perceptual experiences *represent* the world in a certain way, and the *representational content* of the Twins' experiences is the *same*.

This suggestion has to be qualified. To recall, we are planning to analyse internal sameness in terms of the relation between Twins, and then formulate the controversy between internalists and externalists in terms of what internal sameness, and hence standing in this relation, imply: internalists say it implies sameness of mental features, externalists deny this. So, clearly, it has to be common ground between internalists and externalists that Twins stand in this relation. But then we cannot claim that Twins share *all* their mental contents, because this is precisely what externalists deny. A possible solution is to distinguish the 'narrow' and 'broad' content of mental states, and claim that the narrow content of the Twins' thoughts and experiences is the same (for various versions of the distinction, see McGinn 1982; Fodor 1987; Loar 1988; Chalmers 2002).

This account of the Twin situations is not entirely uncontroversial, since the legitimacy of any viable notion of narrow content has been questioned by some defenders of content externalism (e.g., McDowell 1986; Block and Stalnaker 1999). These critics doubt that anything that is recognizably 'content-like' is shared by the Twins either in the Earth/Twin Earth situation, or in the embodied/vat-brain situations. Furthermore, different philosophers envisage the construction of narrow content in rather different ways. If what I said about the meningitis example and about the difficulties in accounting for the relation between the Twins in physical terms is right, then narrow content is not *simply* content that supervenes on internal physical states; but this leaves open a number of questions about its nature.

I shall not offer a separate defence of narrow content, since my own account can be understood as incorporating a certain conception of narrow content. It is part of my account that what it is like to think about wine and what it is like to think about water are different. The intentional features of conscious thoughts are part of their phenomenology. In fact, Horgan, Tienson, Graham, and Loar, who all argue for the extensive understanding of phenomenology that I adopt in my own proposal, see their theories as offering a version of narrow content. In my view, the phenomenally constituted intentional features of thoughts and experiences—their narrow contents, if you like—are shared between Twins, together with all the other phenomenologically constituted features of thoughts and experiences. I defend the notion of phenomenal properties that underlie this proposal in this chapter and the next. In Chapter 7, I shall argue that narrow content so conceived is a genuine version of content, since it can provide truth and reference conditions.

The philosophers who defend the distinction between broad and narrow content—for example, the authors mentioned on the previous page—tend to acknowledge the legitimacy of both. In contrast, I would like to defend an uncompromisingly internalist position: all mental features, and hence all mental *content* features, are internally determined. When I defend the viability of narrow content, this should be understood as the position that all content is narrow.

4.8 Possible Objections to Phenomenal Properties

The suggestion is that the defining feature of Twin situations is that all the Twins' thoughts and experiences share their phenomenal properties (throughout their mental history). I myself think that this is the most intuitive account of the Twin situations, and I am clearly not alone in this. However, the notion of phenomenal properties involved in this suggestion is open to some objections, which need to be answered.

First, I said that, if two experiences involve things 'seeming the same', they have the same phenomenal properties. It has been argued that the notion of phenomenal properties required by this claim is incoherent, since the 'seem the same' relation is not transitive, but the relation of identity of properties—as any relation of identity—should be transitive (see Dummett 1970: 268; Everett 1996).

Secondly, it has to be a common ground between externalists and internalists that the experiences of Twins are indistinguishable, since they define their disagreement in terms of their verdict about the Twin situations. If my account of their relation is right, the Twin experiences share their phenomenal properties. An externalist will then say that, even though the phenomenal characters are the same, the representational or intentional contents are different—Oscar's experience represents H_2O, Twin Oscar's experience represents XYZ. This involves a separation between the phenomenal and intentional features of experiences. However, some defenders of the so-called representational theories of perception *identify* the phenomenal character with the intentional content of experiences. On these views, *all* mental features of a perceptual experience are to be understood in terms of what these experiences represent. The phenomenal character of experience is given by how things seem to the subject, and seemings are characterized in terms of their contents. If this view is combined with content externalism—as, for example, in the case of Fred Dretske (1995) or Micheal Tye (1995)—then we get the result that it seems to Oscar that he is tasting *water*, while it seems to Twin Oscar that he is tasting *twater*, and therefore the contents of seemings, and hence the phenomenal characters, are different.

The classical Twin Earth arguments aim to establish externalism about content; but there are also positions that extend the externalist claim to other mental features. For example, Timothy Williamson (2000) defends externalism about certain propositional attitudes. The third challenge to my notion of phenomenal sameness could be coming from certain defenders of yet another version of externalism about the mental: the disjunctive theory of perception, as defended, for example, by John McDowell (1982) and M. G. F. Martin

(2004, 2005). Disjunctivists claim that, in a pair of situations like the one I described above, about seeing and hallucinating about a teacup, the most specific mental kind exemplified by the veridical perception (VP) is *different* from the most specific mental kind of a corresponding hallucination (H). Since it is generally agreed that a subject could be in the same internal state in an actual VP and a counterfactual H (or the other way around), disjunctivism is a form of externalism about the mental. Of course, internalists would agree that there is *some* difference between a VP and a corresponding H; for example, the presence of an object; but they would insist that this difference does not pertain to the *mental* nature of these experiences.

Disjunctivism comes in several versions. On one version, disjunctivists need not deny that a VP and a corresponding H share their phenomenal character, but they would insist that there is some further mental difference between the two states. For example, one could adopt Williamson's view (2000) that knowing is a mental state that is different from mere believing, and say that a given VP constitutes knowing, while a corresponding H does not, and hence there is a mental difference between the two experiences; but they can still have the same phenomenal properties.

There is, however, a more uncompromising version. One of the frequently mentioned tenets of the disjunctive view is that a certain traditional view of experience is mistaken. According to the traditional view, we have a uniform explanation of what is going on in the case of a VP and a corresponding H—and in cases in general where things seem the same—by appealing to a 'Common Factor'—that is, a mental type that is shared by the two experiences. In contrast, the disjunctivist claims that, in McDowell's words, 'an appearance that such-and-such is the case can be *either* a mere appearance, *or* the fact that such an such is the case making itself perceptually manifest to someone' (McDowell 1982: 211). So appearances have disjunctive explanations, as cases either of perceptions or of hallucinations, hence the name 'disjunctivism' (see also Martin 2004, 2005). Now it seems to me that a view that acknowledged the shared phenomenal character of a VP and the corresponding H could offer a uniform account for the 'appearance that such-and-such is the case' in the two experiences, by appealing to the shared phenomenal character. This would make rather significant allowances to the anti-disjunctivist theory in its recognition of the robustness, and the explanatory power, of the Common Factor. So I assume that an uncompromising disjunctivist would reject that a VP and an H have the *same* phenomenal properties.

I have to add that the three objections I listed above have different motivations, so the objectors may not agree among each other. For example, Michael Tye, who is an externalist representationalist, is explicit in his rejection of the disjunctivist idea that a VP and a corresponding H are phenomenally different. It is instructive to quote what he says in length:

> These comments assume, of course, that the visual experience you have when you see the surfaces is of a kind that could have occurred even if you were hallucinating. And some philosophers (so-called 'disjunctivists') deny that there is any such experience common to perception and hallucination. But while there is certainly *a* difference between one's state of mind in seeing a table, say, and one's state of mind in hallucinating a table—after all, seeing a table is a mental state involving a relation between the subject and a real table—intuitively, there is also something important in common. Intuitively, the reason why one may *think* that one is seeing a flat, square surface not only when one is seeing such a surface but also when one is hallucinating is that one can have a visual experience of the same phenomenal type in both cases.
>
> This seems to me unquestionably the common sense view of the matter. And it is also the view taken by scientists studying the psychology of vision. In scientific work, it is taken for granted that the same conscious visual state can occur whether or not the cells on the retina are activated by light reflected from a seen object or by artificial stimulation. This is reflected both in experimental designs and in the psychological generalizations scientists adduce that cover both veridical visual states and misperceptions alike. (Tye 2002: 140)

I could not agree more. And it seems to me that the scientific results could equally support the idea that one has the same conscious experience whether the cells on the retina are activated by light reflected from water or twater, contrary to what Tye's own view implies. Moreover, I think the 'common sense view of the matter' would say the same about the situation of Oscar and his Twin: intuitively, there is something common to their cases—namely, the phenomenal type of their experiences. It will take some work, however, to substantiate this intuition.

4.9 Externalism About the Phenomenal

The notion of the Twin situations is based on a simple thought. This is the thought that I could be in situations that were indistinguishable from my present situation, and yet various things were different both inside and outside me. Some of the chemical compounds inside and outside my body could be different, I could be on another planet that looks very similar to this one, the objects I take myself to be perceiving could be missing, I could even be a vat brain in a computer world—and yet things could seem exactly the same. These possibilities are, I believe, fundamental to our understanding of the nature of our mind, of our experience, and of empirical knowledge, so any theory of these matters should have a place for these possibilities.

Moreover, I have suggested that this is the key to understanding what lies at the bottom of the internalism/externalism controversy. The internalist thesis is that subjects in Twin situations share all their mental features, and externalists deny this.

My own suggestion is that we should characterize the Twin situations in terms of shared phenomenal properties of conscious thought and experience. In the previous section, we saw that this can be challenged from at least three directions: by those who worry about the non-transitivity of the 'seems-the-same' relation, by defenders of an externalist representationalist view of perception, and by defenders of a certain uncompromising disjunctivist view of perception.

Mental features are commonly classified into phenomenal and intentional features. Externalism in its classical variety is about intentional features, and it seems compatible with the view that phenomenology is internal. Externalist representationalism and the uncompromising version of disjunctivism challenge even this refuge of internalism. It is not only that meanings 'ain't in the head', but, as Alex Byrne and Michael Tye (2006) put in their defence of externalist representationalism, 'qualia ain't in the head' either. The mental states of subjects who participate in the Twin situations differ with respect not only to their intentional, but also to their phenomenological, features.[2]

But then surely these theories owe us an explanation of what makes the Twin situations what they are. As we have seen, the point is not whether things are 'in the head' or not. But, if not physical, functional, or behavioural sameness, not shared narrow content, and not even shared phenomenal character, then *what* makes two situations count as subjectively indistinguishable?

I think the best option for these theories is to develop an *epistemic* analysis of this relation, as, for example, M. G. F. Martin (2004, 2005) explicitly suggested in his defence of disjunctivism. Since the development of this idea will occupy the next chapter, let me just give a brief initial characterization. We could say that Oscar's situation is *indiscriminable* from Twin Oscar's situation, where this

[2] Ned Block (1996) says that the externalist representationalist ('representationist' on his terminology) could distinguish between representational features of the water experiences that do contribute to the phenomenal character, and those that do not. In the first group, there would be features like 'represented as colourless, tasteless, a liquid'; in the second group 'represented as water or twater'. Then the externalist representationalist can claim that Twin experiences share their phenomenal character by sharing the representational features belonging to the first group, but not necessarily those in the second group.

If an externalist representationalist accepts this answer, my project is spared from the objection that the phenomenology of the Twin experiences is not the same. However, I am not sure that the externalist representationalist could, or indeed would, accept this solution for the water case; and if Tye and Byrne's insistence that 'qualia ain't in the head' is to be taken seriously, then they certainly would not accept it as a general solution covering every type of indistinguishable Twin situation.

is understood as an epistemic relation: that Oscar could not tell the two situations apart, or that, for all he knows, he could be in Twin Oscar's situation.

If we accept *my* proposal that Twin experiences have the same phenomenal character, this has a straightforward consequence for the discriminability of certain features of the two situations: since everything is indiscriminable from itself, and since the phenomenal character of the two experiences is the *same*, the phenomenal character of Oscar's actual experience is indiscriminable from the phenomenal character of his counterfactual Twin experience. The two experiences can be different in other respects—for example, with respect to their subject, location, time, physical composition—and it may be possible to discriminate them in these respects. But, surely, the two experiences are indiscriminable with respect to their phenomenal character. The metaphysical conception thus has this automatic epistemic consequence; automatic, because it merely follows from the reflexive nature of the indiscriminability relation.

However, there is no obvious entailment in the other direction. It is true that, since everything is indiscriminable from itself, if Oscar's counterfactual situation is indiscriminable from Oscar's actual situation, then both situations will have the property 'indiscriminable from Oscar's actual situation'. But notice that the epistemic characterization does not commit one to the sameness of any further interesting properties between the two situations—for example, to the sameness of phenomenal character, or of intentional content. And therefore it would suit the purposes of those who want to be externalist even about phenomenology.

However, in the next chapter I shall argue that externalists cannot account for the Twin situations in purely epistemic terms.

5

INDISCRIMINABILITY

5.1 The Fitting Relation

The plan in this chapter is to assess the externalist's prospects of giving an epistemic account of the relation that is constitutive of the Twin situations. The need to give such an account arose for those externalist theories that could not explain subjective indistinguishability in terms of physical, functional, or behavioural sameness, or in terms of shared narrow content, and not even in terms of shared phenomenal character. The remaining option was to offer an epistemic account for the Twin situations—that is, for the situations involving Oscar and his Twin Earth or vat-brain counterpart, or for the situations involving a veridical perception and a corresponding hallucination. I shall argue that there is no such account available for externalists.

So far I have used the terms 'subjective indistinguishability' or 'things seeming the same' interchangeably to characterize this relation, but let me now fix the terminology. I shall assume that I am right about the phenomenon, and that there is a relation here worth analysing. Simply to talk about the relation in neutral terms, I shall often say that two situations or two experiences *fit*, and the relation between them is *fitting* (while 'matching' would perhaps be more natural, it has been used by Nelson Goodman (1951) in a specific sense to which I do not want to commit myself).

This chapter draws on material presented in Farkas (2006), where I focus mainly on the VP/H cases. The present discussion focuses more on the Earth/Twin Earth situations, and tries to clarify or complement my previous arguments.

Sometimes philosophers use 'seems the same' and 'indiscriminable' as synonyms. I shall follow a different course; since there is more than one way to understand the fitting relation, I shall use these expressions to convey the different interpretations. The locutions 'looks (appears, feels, etc.) *the same*' or 'qualitatively *the same*' suggest that something is *identical* in two experiences, and therefore are suitable for expressing the more metaphysically loaded notion of sameness of phenomenal character. The term 'indiscriminable' does not directly have such an implication, but it has more obvious cognitive connotations; so I shall use it to denote the epistemic interpretations of the fitting relation. Since I stipulate that 'looks the same' means 'there is a look that is the same (identical)', the same-look relation, like the relation of identity, is transitive. As we shall see, the same is not true for certain versions of the indiscriminability relation (for discussion of the same issues, though with different terminology, see Graff 2001 and Mills 2002).

I shall analyse three notions of indiscriminability, and argue that, given externalism, none of them is suitable for a purely epistemic characterization of the fitting relation.

5.2 Active Discriminability

The first notion of discrimination I borrow from Timothy Williamson (1990: 7): 'to discriminate between *a* and *b* is to activate knowledge that *a* and *b* are distinct'. Things are indiscriminable if one cannot activate knowledge that they are distinct. I shall call this understanding of discriminability and its cognates 'active'.[1]

Since active discrimination involves a judgement concerning some objects, these objects have to be presented to the

[1] In Farkas (2006), I distinguish another version of active discriminability, suggested by Diana Raffman (2001). Raffman's notion is importantly different from that of Williamson, but not, I hope, in a way to make a difference to the present discussion, so I have simplified the issue by considering only Williamson's version.

The following discussion is greatly indebted to Williamson's analysis (1990, 2000), especially on the issue of the presentation sensitivity of discrimination, even though I eventually depart from Williamson in some of my final conclusions.

discriminating subject *under some presentation*. There is no need to commit ourselves on the nature of these presentations: they could, for example, be Fregean modes of presentations (Frege 1892), or what are called 'guises' by certain opponents of Fregean senses (e.g., Salmon 1986). But the question of presentations is crucial, for, in general, the possibility of active discrimination depends on the way the objects of discrimination are presented: things may be discriminable under one presentation, but not under another. The colour of two vases may be discriminable in broad daylight, but not in the dusk. Someone may be able to discriminate her father from Prince Charles under the modes of presentation 'my father' and 'Prince Charles', but not under the presentations 'that man standing in the corner with his back to me' and 'Prince Charles'—in a case where the man standing there, unbeknownst to her, is her father, but looks rather like Prince Charles from a distance.

Active discriminability also depends on the source of knowledge we activate in discrimination. Suppose I have evidence that two sections have different lengths based on using a sophisticated measuring device, but I do not have evidence for the difference from unaided vision. Then the sections are perceptually indiscriminable, but discriminable with the help of the measuring device.

Let me note a few features of the active indiscriminability relation. First, it is reflexive: since a is not distinct from a, no one can activate knowledge that a is distinct from a. Secondly, once we fix the way the objects of discrimination are presented, the relation is symmetrical. If I cannot activate knowledge that a, presented by M, is distinct from b, presented by N, then I also cannot activate knowledge that b, presented by N, is distinct from a, presented by M. However, of course this allows that a and b would be discriminable under some other presentations.

Thirdly, active indiscriminability is non-transitive. A simple example to illustrate this: a man is standing in the far end of the hall with his back to you, who could be either your friend Ned or your friend Ted; you cannot discriminate him from Ned, and you cannot discriminate Ted from him, but you can, of course, discriminate Ned from Ted. Another type of case will deserve special attention later, so let me describe it in a bit more detail.

Imagine the experience of watching the hour hand of the clock. For the sake of simplicity, I shall imagine a clock that has only an hour hand, and the minute hand is missing. For sufficiently short periods of times, I cannot perceptually discriminate the position of the hand from the position it occupied before. Yet, after some time, the movement of the hand becomes noticeable. We may enquire about the perceptual discrimination of the position of the hand; but we can also make a point about trying *introspectively to discriminate* our *visual experiences*. We have the following series:

- at 3.00.00 I have a visual experience of the hour hand pointing at 3;
- at 3.00.05 I have a visual experience I cannot introspectively discriminate from my visual experience at 3.00.00;
- at 3.00.10 I have a visual experience I cannot introspectively discriminate from my visual experience at 3.00.05;

  ...
- at 3.15.00 I have a visual experience I *can* introspectively discriminate from my visual experience at 3.00.00.

The position the hand appears to occupy at 3.15 is different from the position it appears to occupy at 3.00. Since the phenomenal character experience is characterized by the way things appear, this means the experiences' characters are different, and I can activate knowledge that they are. However, each of the experiences at 5-second intervals was indiscriminable from the previous one; as far as I could judge, the hand appeared to occupy the same position as it did 5 seconds before. So we have a series of experiences, where the adjacent experiences are introspectively indiscriminable, but the first and the last are introspectively discriminable.

A series like this—where the phenomenal character of experiences imperceptibly changes until the changes add up to a noticeable difference—is called a 'phenomenal sorites' series. Another example of a phenomenal sorites series is watching a series of slides that turn imperceptibly from blue to purple. We cannot discriminate the colour experience of any slide from the colour experience of the previous one, yet we can discriminate the colour experience of the first slide from that of the last slide. Yet another example is someone's feeling cold in the morning and gradually warming up, again, through imperceptible changes.

The phenomenal sorites series is the basis of the first objection I mentioned in Section 4.8 against my notion of phenomenal properties. According to the objection, what happens, say, in the hour-hand case, is that the position the hand *appears to occupy* is the *same* as the position it appeared to occupy 5 seconds before. Within 5 seconds, everything *seems the same* when we look at the clock. This, however, would mean that the *phenomenal properties* of the visual experience also remain the *same*. This is true throughout the 15 minutes we are dealing with; and, since identity is transitive, the phenomenal properties of the first experience should be the same as the those of the last. But they are clearly not.

This objection is based on the initially plausible, but ultimately incorrect, claim that, *if we cannot discriminate the way two things look, then they look the same*. I shall explain in Section 5.6 how matters stand with this issue.

Let me state once more what the project is. My own proposal is that the class of situations that fit my present situation are precisely those situations where I have an experience with the same phenomenal properties as my present experience. On the alternative, purely epistemic characterization of the fitting relation, we try to dispense with the idea that the two experiences have the same phenomenal character. As we saw, one motivation for this may be that some theories—like externalist representationalism—would deny that Twin experiences have the same phenomenal character, so, if they wanted to account for the fitting relation, they would have to characterize it in different terms. In this case, indiscriminability is not the consequence of sameness of phenomenal character, but must be understood independently;

and the claim is that the situations that fit my present situations are precisely those that I cannot actively discriminate from my present situation.

5.3 Reflective Knowledge

Active discriminability depends on how the objects of discrimination are presented, and on the evidence we take into account. Consequently, we have to specify the objects of discrimination, their presentation, and the source of evidence for the potential discriminating judgement.

Let us begin with the evidence. Suppose that someone is told by a very trustworthy source that she is about to undergo a hallucination as part of a psychological experiment. The experimenters induce a perfect hallucination; by normal standards of knowledge, the subject knows—based on testimony and memory—that she is not having a veridical perception. Yet the hallucination is a hallucination, and still subjectively indistinguishable from a veridical perception (whatever that means). When we talk about our inability to distinguish the *subjectively* indistinguishable Twin situations, this is understood as saying that we have no evidence from *reflection* or *introspection*, that certain experiences are distinct.

This gives us at least one immediate reason to doubt that we can capture the fitting relation in terms of active indiscriminability: that it makes it unintelligible how a creature who does not have the capacity of reflective knowledge can have fitting experiences. It seems that a cat, for example, could have a VP and it would be physiologically possible to induce a corresponding H; but these would not be fitting experiences for the cat *because* it cannot reflectively discriminate them. The cat cannot reflectively discriminate *any two* of its experiences, even those with very different characters, simply because it cannot reflectively discriminate, period.[2]

[2] Susanna Siegel presents this criticism against M. G. F. Martin's account of hallucination as an experience that is indiscriminable from veridical perceptions (Siegel 2004, reflecting

Generalizing this point, the inability to discriminate between two experiences can be a result of a cognitive deficiency that has nothing to do with the character of experiences. On my theory, the cat can have fitting experiences, because it can have experiences with the same phenomenal character. For creatures like ourselves, who are endowed with the ability of reflective discrimination, fitting experiences will, of course, be indiscriminable with respect to their phenomenal character.

One way out of this problem would be an insistence that human perceptual experience is fundamentally different from animal experience—for example, because it is permeated by concepts. If so, then perhaps it is acceptable to have an application of the fitting relation only to our experiences. However, I would like to show that, even on this assumption, active indiscriminability is unsuitable for accounting for the fit between two experiences.

Reflective discriminability of experiential features can be tested best when the features the subject compares are both presented experientially at the same time, and hence the subject can reflect directly on both of them. Direct comparison is not available for the Twin situations. One cannot have a VP and an H (of the same thing) at the same time; nor can one be on Earth and Twin Earth at the same time. This is actually a crucial point. We have to assume that the subject, Oscar, is in *one* of the situations, which is presented to him as 'my current situation', and, by reflecting on the features of his current experience, he attempts to discriminate it from other experiences, which are presented to him in some way other than being directly experienced; most plausibly by some description, or through memory. The tricky question is how the other situations should be presented.

on Martin 2004). Martin (2005) returns to the issue with an account that appeals to idealized cognizers. But the question of how an idealized cognizer could have the very same kind of experiences as the cat has remains problematic.

5.4 The Importance of Presentations

As I said, the active indiscriminability of objects depends on how they are presented to the subject. This is really important, because, if we claim that a subject cannot actively discriminate between *a* and *b*, we have not given a proper account of what it is exactly that she does not know, unless we specify how *a* and *b* are presented to her. The following example will help to illustrate this.

The story of Oscar and his Twin is usually told by describing the situation from *our* point of view: *we* conceive Oscar's situation as the actual one with H_2O, and contrast it with a counterfactual situation involving XYZ, or with his Twin's situation on another planet, and claim that he cannot discriminate one from the other. However, this description does not reveal what it is exactly that Oscar does not know (assuming that the relevant notion of indiscriminability is active indiscriminability, and hence depends on how the objects of discrimination are presented). For, if Oscar presented to himself the situations in a similar fashion, then he should be asking the following questions:

> How do I know that this experience I am having is not a counterfactual experience, which I don't have, but could have had, should I have been brought up in a different environment? Or how do I know that the experience I am having of this stuff, is not some different experience some other bloke is having of another stuff at another part of the universe?

Put this way, nothing is easier than to answer these questions: of course, the experience he is having is not the experience he is not having—the experiences presented as 'the actual experience' and 'a counterfactual experience that differs from the actual experience in some way' are different by definition, so he *can* activate knowledge that they are different.

If we want to capture what it is that Oscar does not know, we have to find a more appropriate presentation of the other situation. To begin with, the question is not whether Oscar can discriminate the *particular* experience event he is undergoing from other experience events; the question concerns the *kind* of experience he is having. So perhaps the idea is something like this: Oscar can identify various features of his current experience by reflection—for example, that the water he is drinking feels ice cold. Therefore he can discriminate his current experience from other experience types that involve, say, drinking tepid water. But there is no reflectively revealed feature of his experience that would teach him that he is not drinking XYZ. The relevant statement of Oscar's ignorance would be this (italics include the objects of discrimination): 'I cannot activate reflective knowledge that *my present experience* is not *an experience of drinking XYZ*.'

We assume Oscar is chemically ignorant, so this is true; and, even if he were chemically knowledgeable, he could not find out that the stuff he is drinking is not XYZ merely by reflection. The suggestion would be this: since Twin experiences are instances of a type of experience ('drinking XYZ') that Oscar cannot discriminate from his present experience, they fit Oscar's present experience. But this will not do. Here is another piece of Oscar's ignorance: 'I cannot activate reflective knowledge that *my present experience* is not *an experience of drinking* $C_2H_4O_2$.'

But, as a matter of fact, drinking acetic acid ($C_2H_4O_2$) is subjectively very different from drinking water. The relation that we said intuitively holds between drinking water and twater, but not between drinking water and wine, does not hold between drinking water and acetic acid either. So merely being an instance of a type of experience that Oscar cannot discriminate from his current experience is not a sufficient condition for a fit between the two experiences.

A similar problem would arise with respect to the VP/H Twin situations. It may be suggested that VPs are indiscriminable from Hs in virtue of the fact that, when Oscar is having an H, he cannot know he is not having a VP, and consequently, he can truly say: 'I cannot activate reflective knowledge that *my current experience* is not *a veridical perception*.' This may be true. The problem is that 'veridical perception' covers all sorts of experiences that clearly do not fit Oscar's current experience. We cannot say: being an instance of the type of experience ('veridical perception') is necessary and sufficient for a fit with Oscar's current experience.

These examples show that saying that 'an experience is reflectively indiscriminable from my present experience' is too unspecific to capture what is special about experiences that fit my present experience. We can probably find *some* presentation for *any* experience that would make it impossible to discriminate it from my current experience. The requirement that a fitting experience should be indiscriminable from my current experience under *some* presentation is too weak; we should try to strengthen it.

5.5 Successive Presentations

Twin situations cannot be directly compared in one experience. But perhaps we could try to get as close to the direct experiential comparison of experiences as possible by exposing the subject to the two different experiences in immediate succession. So consider all the possible sequences when Oscar has a VP and then a corresponding H. In both cases, the features of the experience are presented to him through being directly experienced, and hence available for reflection. In each of these cases, he will have to say 'I cannot activate reflective knowledge that *this experience* is different from *that experience*', where 'that experience' refers to his previous VP. (Obviously, the comparison is between kinds of experiences; the particular events can be discriminated by the time of their occurrence.) A similar statement would apply to all the sequences where Oscar has first a water-drinking experience followed by a fitting twater-drinking experience: he will not be able to activate reflective knowledge that the second (presented as 'this experience') is different from the first (presented as 'that experience').

The suggestion is then this: two experiences fit, if, and only if, all the sequences of first having the first type of experience, and then having the other type of experience, would leave the subject unable to activate reflective knowledge that 'this experience' (referring to the second) is different from 'that experience' (referring to the first).

All Twin experiences satisfy this condition (which has a neat explanation if my theory of the fitting relation is correct: it is the result of the experiences having the same phenomenal character). However, the defender of the purely epistemic approach has the following worry to face: that there could still be an experience that was subjectively different from Oscar's current experience, and yet satisfied this condition. First, suppose that Oscar has a water-drinking experience, followed by a delirious experience of scary monsters, which affects him so much that he completely forgets the water-drinking experience he had before. In this case, he cannot activate reflective knowledge that 'this experience' (of the monsters) is different from 'that experience' (drinking water). Yet the experiences obviously do not fit (see Siegel 2004).

It may be suggested that, if we took into account *all* the sequences of first having the water-drinking experience and then having the scary-monster experience, some of these sequences would have no memory loss, and the subject could activate knowledge that the experiences are different. But I do not see why this should apply to every possible case. We can imagine, for example, an experience of a magical object that is jinxed in such a way that everyone who ever has this experience immediately forgets about it; and, once one is in the presence of the magical object, one is so awed that one cannot recall other type of experiences. In this case, all experiences would be reflectively indiscriminable from this magical experience, even though they would not fit. The possibility, though obviously not actual, is perfectly intelligible. This, I claim, is explained by the fact that we have a prior understanding of the fitting relation in terms of similarity of phenomenal characters.

The point is related to the cat case: there is a cognitive deficiency that prevents the subject from activating knowledge of the distinctness of experiences. In the case of the cat, the deficiency is the general lack of ability to acquire reflective knowledge; in this case, the deficiency is the memory loss; but neither deficiency has anything to do with the fitting relation.

5.6 Phenomenal Similarity and Phenomenal Sameness

It may be suggested that, in spite of all that has been said, we do have a good model for understanding how subsequent experiences may *not* be the *same* phenomenally, and yet fit in a sense that could satisfy the intuitions about the fitting relation: the adjacent members of the phenomenal sorites series. We cannot claim that the adjacent members of the phenomenal sorites have the same phenomenal character, since, if they did, then the first and the last should have the same phenomenal character, which they clearly do not. Yet the adjacent experiences seem to satisfy the condition specified above: successive experiences of their type would leave the subject unable to activate reflective knowledge that 'this experience' (referring to the second) is different from 'that experience' (referring to the first).[3] Now the suggestion may be that a water-drinking experience and a fitting twater-drinking experience are related to each other in the same way as the adjacent members of the phenomenal sorites series are; the same is true of a VP and the corresponding H.

This suggestion would appear to assume that the relation between adjacent members of the phenomenal sorites series is *simply* reflective indiscriminability. I do not think that this assumption is correct. The visual experiences of successive colour patches are *phenomenally very similar.* That is, there is some determinable phenomenal property whose determinate values are organized into a (possibly multi-dimensional) scale along similarity relations, and these two experiences exhibit phenomenal properties that are very close to

[3] Williamson (1990) argues that, if the phenomenal characters really are different, then there would be experiential presentations where the characters are actively discriminable. I am not convinced that this is right; but, if it is, then it is easier to make my case, since in that case the phenomenal sorites cannot be used as a model for the fitting relation; I assume the idea is that difference between a VP and a corresponding H can *never* be detected.

each other on this scale. It is *almost the same* shade of blue; almost the same degree of cold; almost the same apparent position of the clock hand. The reason why we cannot discriminate them is that they are so very similar, and our ability to retain exact phenomenal detail in memory is limited.

This limitation on our memory will be familiar to everyone who has ever tried to compare tastes, for example, at a wine tasting. When I have the taste of one wine, the experience is present in all its completely determinate phenomenal specificity, to the exclusion of all others; but, as soon as the experience is gone, the details immediately fade from reflective consciousness, and what we retain in memory for comparative purposes is less specific.

It is said that our discriminatory capacities are limited, in the sense that small physical differences in shades of colours or lengths are not reflected in a difference of the phenomenal properties of our experiences of them. 'Physics is finer than the eye,' as Charles Travis puts it (Travis 1985: 350). An equally important and unavoidable limitation of our discriminative powers has to do with our limited ability to retain completely specific phenomenal information. Direct experiential presentation is finer than memory. Therefore the principle 'if we cannot discriminate the way things appear, then they appear the same' is false, at least in cases when discrimination concerns successive experiences.

This circumstance explains the possibility, indeed the inevitability, of the temporal phenomenal sorites cases. The adjacent members are phenomenally very similar; so much so that their difference is lost in the transition from one experience to the other; hence our inability to discriminate. But I would like to insist that our understanding of such a series is based primarily on the idea of phenomenally very similar experiences, and indiscriminability is added as a consequence. If the series was merely a series of pairwise indiscriminable experiences, with the first discriminable from the last, we could have some series with magical experiences. The phenomenal sorites series is clearly different—because we conceive it as a series of phenomenally very similar experiences.

So I do not think we can get away from references to phenomenal character and their similarity, and capture the fitting relation in purely epistemic terms. And this points to some problems with the idea that we could conceive the relation between Twin experiences to be the same as the relation between the adjacent members of the phenomenal sorites series. The idea under consideration is this: a water-drinking experience and a twater-drinking experience are phenomenally very similar, though not identical, just like feelings of cold with almost identical intensity, or almost identical apparent shades of blue, which constitute adjacent members of the sorites.

This analogy is problematic though, at least for two reasons. First, in the case of the phenomenal sorites, the adjacent members are slightly differing determinate values of a determinable phenomenal property. Prima facie, there is no such phenomenal determinable in the case of water and twater: what is the phenomenal property that can come in a water shade and a twater shade, or in a water intensity and a twater intensity? In fact, the only way of making sense of the idea that water and twater experiences are phenomenally very similar is to conceive them as having almost the same *apparent colour* (perhaps twater is just an indiscriminable shade more coloured than water), almost the same *taste* (twater with just an indiscriminable pinch of sourness), almost the same smell, temperature, and so on. But this means that we have a grasp of the phenomenal character of these experiences that is *independent from the representational features of one seeming to be water, the other seeming to be twater.* If so, then there is no theoretical obstacle to stipulating that they have *exactly the same*, rather than *almost the same*, colour, taste, smell, and so on.

This point is reinforced by all the common descriptions of the Twin Earth cases. Being told that the stuff Twin Oscar calls 'water' is XYZ rather than H_2O gives us no proper idea of the situation; it is the fact that XYZ is colourless, odourless, tasteless, quenches thirst—in other words, appears the same as water—that conveys the appropriate idea. And, when we are told they are indistinguishable, we automatically imagine this as having the same or similar familiar phenomenal properties.

In any case, and this is a further crucial point, it would be odd for an *externalist* representationalist to claim that the phenomenal character of water and twater are different, though very close, *in the same way* as in the case of the adjacent members of the sorites series. The changes in phenomenal character as we proceed along the sorites series involve *internal* changes, both physically and phenomenally. There are internal physical changes if we want to get from a visual experience of blue to a visual experience of purple; if we 'freeze' the internal physical state of the subject while showing a series of colour patches, we cannot expect that her experiences will change. And, of course, there are phenomenal changes too, if we want to get gradually from the first phenomenal character to the last. In that case, however, *an internalist could wholeheartedly agree* that the content of these experiences are different. An internalist should not have a problem with saying that, when there is a difference between the phenomenal character of two visual experiences of the clock's hand, the experiences represent the hand as being in different positions, even if ever so slightly. Similarly, an internalist would find it natural to say that, when there is a difference in the apparent shades of blue that characterize two experiences, the colour of the patches is represented as being just a tiny bit different.

So the analogy with the adjacent members of the phenomenal sorites will not deliver the purely epistemic understanding of the fitting relation that suits the externalist understanding of phenomenal properties. The upshot of this discussion is that we cannot account for the fitting relation in terms of active indiscriminability for reasons presented in Sections 5.3 to 5.5, and trying to conceive the relation between Twin experiences on the model of the phenomenal sorites series will not help this project either. (I present additional considerations, focusing on the VP/H scenarios, in Farkas 2006.)

5.7 Access Indiscriminability

The conclusion of the previous sections was that active indiscriminability is not suitable for characterizing the relation between Twin situations. However, there are other ways to understand the notion of indiscriminability. When talking about indiscriminability, people often say that a situation *A* is indiscriminable from situation *B*, if, when the subject is in *A*, *for all she knows*, she could be in *B*. This phrase is actually ambiguous. On the one hand, it could be—and it often is—understood as simply another way of characterizing active discrimination. The subject is on Earth, and she is wondering whether she is on Twin Earth, which is presented to her in a certain way. She cannot activate knowledge that she is not in the situation thus presented, so, we might say, for all she knows, she could be in it.

There is, however, another understanding, and this takes us to our *second* concept of discrimination. Take all the propositions the subject knows in a certain situation *A*. If all these propositions are true in a situation *B*, then, for all she knows, the subject could be in *B*. It is a situation not ruled out by whatever she knows. I shall also say that situation *B* is 'epistemically accessible' from situation *A*. Assuming that 'not indiscriminable' implies 'discriminable', a situation is discriminable from the subject's present situation if it is ruled out by her knowledge; it is one that is incompatible with something she knows. I shall call this sense of discrimination and its cognates '*access* discrimination'.[4]

There are a number of differences between the 'active' and the 'access' conception. Active discriminability is very general: any two things can be objects of active discrimination, neither of

[4] I drew the idea of interpreting discrimination along these lines from Williamson (2000). Williamson does characterize discrimination in terms of 'for all one knows' (e.g., p. 45); and does use 'for all one knows' to denote the relation of epistemic accessibility described here (e.g., p. 224). Yet I hesitate to attribute this notion to Williamson, since it is, as I argue below, different from his explicitly endorsed notion of active discrimination.

which needs to be one's present situation. In contrast, the objects of access indiscriminability are always one's present situation and some other situation. Furthermore, we saw that *active* discrimination is presentation sensitive, and hence a claim that a subject can actively discriminate between two objects makes sense only relative to some presentation, and thus requires that there *is* such a presentation for *both objects*. But access discrimination does not seem to require this, as the following example will illustrate.

Suppose the subject is standing in Trafalgar Square, and she knows she is facing a tall column with a statue on the top. Then it is not true that, for all she knows, she could be in Kossuth Square in Budapest, for there is no such column in Kossuth Square, so the subject could not be facing one. Something is known in the first situation that is incompatible with her being in the second situation. Yet this will be true of a subject who, standing in Trafalgar Square, has never heard of Kossuth Square, and hence Kossuth Square is presented to her in no way whatsoever. Crucially, for the other situation not to be epistemically accessible from her present one, she does not need to *know* that some known proposition is false there; it is enough if the proposition *is* false there.

Of course, what she knows in the first situation (in Trafalgar Square) depends on how *that* situation is presented to her (for example, whether it is day or night). It is also possible that she has some knowledge of Kossuth Square, which is consequently presented to her in some way. Perhaps she knows that Kossuth Square is not in Britain, whereas she herself is; in this case her knowledge of Kossuth Square rules out her being there. However, once her knowledge in the first situation is fixed, there can be only *one* verdict concerning another situation: it is either discriminable or not from her present situation, and its discriminability does not *vary* according to its presentations.

Not so with active discrimination. Suppose the subject's predicament is as before, and also that she cannot activate knowledge that Trafalgar Square is distinct from the place where her father proposed to her mother. (To put it more simply: she does not know whether the proposal took place in Trafalgar Square.) In fact, the proposal took place in Kossuth Square. Then the situation of standing in Kossuth Square, presented as 'standing in the square where Father proposed to Mother', is not actively discriminable from her present situation. But it is not true that, for all she knows, she could be there.

We can also compare the logical features of the active and access indiscriminability relations. Access indiscriminability is reflexive: everything the subject knows is true in her present situation. It is not transitive: suppose the subject knows only p and q in A; p and q are true in B, but the subject only knows p; in C, p is true and q is false. Then B is access indiscriminable from A, and C from B, but not C from A. However, access indiscriminability, unlike active indiscriminability, is *not symmetrical.* Some of the most interesting cases of lack of symmetry have to do with various sceptical hypotheses. The anti-sceptic should hold that the epistemic access between the normal world and the brain-in-a-vat world is not symmetrical. If I know I have hands, I could not, 'for all I know', be a vat brain; there is something I know that would be false if I were a vat brain. However, my vat-brain counterpart, knowing virtually nothing about the world, could, for all she knows, be in the embodied world. So the normal world is access *in*discriminable from the vat world, but the vat world is access discriminable from the normal world (cf. Williamson 2000: sect. 8.2).[5]

Since access indiscriminability does not depend on presentations in the way active discriminability does, the problems we faced in Section 5.4 in trying to find an adequate presentation of the other

[5] The active discriminability/indiscriminability of these situations is symmetrical, once we fix presentations. At the moment, the normal world is presented to me as 'my present situation', and the vat world as 'the vat situation'. If I can (or cannot) activate knowledge that my present situation is distinct from the vat world, I can (or cannot) activate knowledge that the vat world is distinct from my present situation. Hence symmetry. If I were in the vat world, then the presentation of the worlds would change; the vat world would be presented as 'my present situation'. But, once we fix again the presentations, both active discriminability and indiscriminability remain symmetrical.

situation do not emerge. So perhaps we can use it to define the fitting relation.

5.8 Access Indiscriminability and Twin Situations

Let us see now whether access indiscriminability could explain the relation between the Twin situations. Note first that indiscriminability in one direction is not enough: we cannot say that an H fits a VP only in virtue of the H being access indiscriminable from the VP, but not the other way around. Being unconscious, or dreamlessly sleeping, is indiscriminable from all sorts of experiential situations; since the subject does not know anything about her current experiences, she could have a variety of experiences, for all she knows. But the situation of dreamless sleep does not fit a wakeful experiential situation. The remedy is to require that the H is indiscriminable from the VP as well, and, in that case, just as before, we have to constrain the relevant knowledge to reflective or introspective knowledge. As we saw, unless we are sceptics, for all a subject knows *empirically*, she cannot be in the vat-brain situation. The suggestion is instead that, for all she knows from *reflection*, she could be a brain in a vat.

According to a widely accepted view, the contents of thoughts we express by using proper names constitutively depend on their object. Suppose Oscar is thinking about his friend Lucinda, and says to himself, truly and knowledgeably: 'I am now thinking of Lucinda.' Given the widely accepted view, this proposition would not be true in a counterfactual situation where Oscar grows up on Twin Earth, never meets Lucinda, but only Lucinda's Doppelgänger (also called 'Lucinda')—for there he would not be thinking of Lucinda, but rather of Lucinda's Doppelgänger. What he knows on Earth is inconsistent with his being on Twin Earth. The more of an externalist one is, the more pervasive the phenomenon will be. Knowledge of thoughts of natural kinds, thoughts expressible by proper names, indexicals, or on a disjunctivist view, thoughts about experiences, will all constrain the situations in which one could be, for all one knows from reflection. Being on Earth is not reflectively access indiscriminable from being on Twin Earth.

The view that the content of singular thoughts depends constitutively on their objects is a version of externalism. Therefore, the above argument grants to the externalist that one can have reflective knowledge of thoughts with broad content. I am going to question this in Chapter 6, so it may be asked why I think it is legitimate to use it in this argument. First, because it is a claim that most externalists would certainly like to uphold, and I am not sure that they would be prepared to give it up in order to define the fitting relation in terms of access indiscriminability. But suppose that they do give it up; this would actually make my job simpler, since my ultimate aim is to show that externalism is incompatible with privileged access, and, since privileged access is the mark of the mental, externalism is mistaken.

Furthermore, I doubt that giving up reflective knowledge of broad contents would help to capture the fitting relation in terms of access indiscriminability (if externalism is true). If Oscar does not know he is thinking of Lucinda, then it seems that he does not know whom he is thinking of, and then all sorts of situations will be access indiscriminable from his present situation—not only thinking of Twin Lucinda, but also thinking of Melinda or Belinda, situations that do not fit his present situation. Note that we cannot say that such situations are excluded by the fact that he knows he is *not* thinking of Melinda or Belinda, since these thoughts all involve broad contents and he is not supposed to have reflective knowledge of these matters.

A further suggestion may be that we should distinguish between the narrow and broad content of thoughts expressible by proper names, and say that we know reflectively merely the *narrow* content of our thoughts. The narrow content would be shared between Oscar's thoughts of Lucinda and Twin Lucinda, but not between his thoughts of Lucinda and Melinda, so his knowledge of the narrow content would not exclude the first situation, but would exclude the second. However, if we acknowledge that a narrow content is shared between Twin thoughts, the purely epistemic account becomes unnecessary, since we can point to a shared mental feature between the two situations that explains fitting. It is true that the narrow content of a Lucinda-thought is indiscriminable from the narrow content of a Twin Lucinda-thought, but this is merely the familiar consequence of the reflexivity of indiscriminability, and the identity of narrow contents.

A different response to the finding that reflective knowledge of broad contents makes Earth reflectively discriminable from Twin Earth is that, contrary to what seemed initially plausible, being on Earth is actually discriminable from being on Twin Earth. Note that, since, according to the popular view, a vat-brain counterpart of Oscar (one who has been a vat brain all its life) could not be thinking of Lucinda either, being a vat brain would also be discriminable from Oscar's present situation. But then there is no hope that we capture the fitting relation in terms of access indiscriminability, because, as I said above, that would require mutual indiscriminability of situations. So, given externalism about content, access indiscriminability is not suitable for defining the fitting relation.

5.9 Response Discrimination

In this section I discuss the third sense of 'discrimination'. Two types of stimuli—associated with two objects, two kinds, two properties, or the like—are discriminable for a subject in this sense if they *generate different cognitive responses* (see Goldman 1976 and Clark 1993). For example, perceivers like us respond discriminatively to blue and green, because a blue patch and a green patch produce different visual experiences, and those, in turn, produce different judgements about the colour of the patch we are looking at.

This is merely the sketch of the notion, and the details can vary. For example, we may want to specify which type of cognitive response we are particularly interested in—say the visual experience or the ensuing judgement. Or the notion can be put forward as a strict or as a statistical notion. In the latter case, we require the subject to respond discriminatively to different stimuli over a number of trials in a statistically relevant majority of the cases. I am going to call this sense of discrimination '*response* discrimination'. Two objects are response indiscriminable if they produce the same cognitive response.

Response indiscriminability shares some features with access indiscriminability, and differs on these points from active indiscriminability. Considering whether certain situations are response discriminable for me, it is not essential that the situations are presented to me in any way in my current situation; it is still a fact that I would, or would not, produce a different response in those situations. And *how* the possible situations are presented to me (if they are presented at all), may not affect the issue of discriminability. For example, I may not be able actively to discriminate the situations of 'looking at Oscar's favourite colour' and 'looking at Lucinda's favourite colour', since I have no idea what their favourite colours are, and whether they are the same or different. Still, the two situations—as it happens, looking at turquoise and looking at pink—are response discriminable for me. (Of course, just as in the case of access discriminability, my cognitive response may depend on how an object is presented to me in a given situation; say whether it is nearby or far away. However, these specifications are better included in the description of the situation, that is, of the object of discrimination itself.)

Response indiscriminability is based on the identity relation (identity of cognitive responses), hence it is an equivalence relation. So response indiscriminability—like all other varieties of indiscriminability—is reflexive; like active indiscriminability, it is symmetrical, and, unlike either active or access indiscriminability, it is transitive.

The definition of response indiscriminability—unlike the definitions of the other two versions we discussed—does not contain reference to knowledge. This may be an advantage for various purposes. One advantage for a number of philosophers is that the notion is applicable to simpler biological organisms, or even to machines, and hence it lends itself easily to a naturalized explanation (this motivation is clearly present in both Goldman 1976 and Clark 1993). Secondly, it has been suggested that discrimination is a necessary condition for knowledge; if discrimination contains no reference to knowledge, this helps to provide a non-circular condition (see Goldman 1976 again). This can be useful even if one is not particularly interested in a naturalistic explanation. Thirdly, since response discriminability can be applied to creatures who lack the ability of reflective knowledge, it does not face the objection that I brought against the idea of using active indiscriminability to define the fitting relation in Section 5.3. We can make sense of things being response indiscriminable for a cat if it responds, say, with the same visual states to certain stimuli.

However, the attempt to define the fitting relation in terms of response discrimination faces similar problems to the earlier attempt to use access discrimination for this purpose, if externalism about content is accepted. Since the content of first-order thoughts is different in the Twin situations in the externalist view, the subject's cognitive responses to these thoughts, that is, his reflectively formed second-order thoughts, will be different too. We do not even have to take stance on the question of whether one can have reflective *knowledge* of one's thoughts if externalism is true. If Oscar believes he is thinking of Lucinda, this is a belief he would not have if he were brought up on Twin Earth, so his cognitive responses—whether they constitute knowledge or mere belief—are different in the two situations.

In this case, it would not even help to distinguish narrow and broad contents, as long as we assume that we can form second-order thoughts whose content inherits the broad content of certain first-order thoughts. The only way to make the two situations response indiscriminable would be to hold that *all* the thought contents are shared between Oscar and his counterfactual Twin. But in that case, again, we do not need an independent epistemic characterization of the fitting relation, since we could just as well define it as shared contents. And, as in the previous cases, this would have the automatic indiscriminability consequence.

5.10 Conclusions, Internalism Stated

In this chapter I have considered three interpretations of what 'indiscriminability' may mean, and argued that an externalist cannot use either understanding as a basis for defining the fitting relation. My hope is that what people mean by 'indiscriminability' is essentially some version of one of these three interpretations. Though I cannot entirely exclude the possibility that there is some other understanding that did not occur to me, until further notice I hold onto the conclusion that the fitting relation cannot be captured in purely epistemic terms. Instead, I claim, it should be analysed as sameness of phenomenal properties.

Where does this leave the objections that I considered against this analysis? As for the non-transitivity of the 'seems-the-same' relation, I argued that in fact this relation is transitive, and should be distinguished from the active indiscriminability relation, which is indeed non-transitive. Furthermore, I argued that indiscriminability does not entail phenomenal sameness, and I explained this fact by reference to the limitation of our memory in keeping in mind exact phenomenal detail.

What about disjunctivism and externalist representationalism? If I am right so far, then these theories have no resources to account for the intuitive idea that things could be different both inside and outside me, and yet things would seem the same. I regard this as a very serious shortcoming in a theory, and in fact sufficient for a refutation.

It has to be noted though that there is an understanding of externalist representationalism that is immune to the difficulties that I raised in this chapter. One could argue that it is in fact compatible with externalist representationalism that the phenomenal character of the Twins' experiences is the same. According to this suggestion, the important claim in representationalist theories is that intentional content *determines* phenomenal character; or that phenomenal character *supervenes* on intentional content. This makes it impossible to have a phenomenal difference without an intentional difference, but should not necessarily exclude an intentional difference without a phenomenal one. Phenomenal character is not independent of, or is over and above, intentional features; rather it is *one aspect* of the intentional nature of an experience. If it is possible that different intentional contents determine the same phenomenal character, this may be the case on Earth and Twin Earth.

A second remark is that there is a version of disjunctivism, too, that is immune to the problems I raised in this chapter—the 'more compromising' version I mentioned before. This theory can allow that a VP and a corresponding H share their phenomenal character, but would argue that there is an additional mental difference between them.

Now I can state my internalist position in more detail. The general idea was that the notion of the 'internal' that is relevant to the internalism/externalism debate is internality to one's subjective viewpoint, or to one's perspective. 'Internal sameness' thus means that things seem the same or are subjectively indistinguishable for the subject. Internalism about a given mental feature is the view that, as long as things seem the same or are indistinguishable for two subjects (in actual or counterfactual circumstances), they agree in the feature in question.

The need to define the fitting relation in terms of phenomenal sameness showed that one has to be internalist at least about phenomenal character, and that strong externalist theories, which claim that there are no mental features shared by the Twins in Twin situations, are mistaken. (This is also the position occupied by Horgan, Tienson, and Graham, whose work I referenced earlier when introducing the notion of phenomenal properties; see Horgan et al. 2004.) Internalism about a certain mental feature can now be formulated as the view that the phenomenal properties of conscious thoughts and experiences, which are shared between subjects in Twin situations, determine the mental feature in question. Externalism is the denial of this view.

Internalism comes in various strengths, depending on the range of mental features one is an internalist about. I myself believe in internalism in its strongest form: that all mental features are internally determined. This is a strong claim indeed, and one significant part of it I am not going to defend in this book. In Section 2.2 I drew a distinction between mental features that belong to the stream of consciousness, on the one hand, and those belonging to standing states, with propositional attitudes like beliefs and desires as primary examples, on the other. I mentioned two views about these standing states. According to the first, a standing state can pass in and out of the stream of consciousness; according to the second, standing states are essentially non-conscious, and hence cannot enter into the stream of consciousness, but they do have important relations to certain conscious events like judgements or acts of reflection.

Phenomenal properties characterize mental events in the stream of consciousness. A non-conscious state or a state outside the stream of consciousness does not have phenomenal properties. Internalism about all mental features would be the view that phenomenal properties of mental events in the stream of consciousness (throughout the subject's mental history) determine all her mental features, including those outside the stream of consciousness. I find this view plausible, at least in the case of creatures like us, who have a sufficiently rich mental life. For example, even a deeply repressed desire would have its predecessor in some conscious experience, and its consequences in the form of certain feelings. But this is a large issue that I cannot attempt to resolve here. Instead, I will restrict myself to asserting a somewhat more moderate form of internalism: that the phenomenal properties of mental events in the stream of consciousness determine all properties of *these* events. I say 'determine', but I mean in fact 'exhaust'. The mental nature of these events is entirely given by their phenomenal properties, in the extended sense of 'phenomenal' that I introduced in Chapter 4.

Even though this version is moderate compared to the full-blown version of internalism, it is still more internalist than most contemporary views about content. It conflicts with all varieties of externalism mentioned so far. Occurrent thoughts like 'water is wet' or 'Descartes was a great philosopher' are part of the stream of consciousness, and they have content; hence, according to content externalists, these thoughts have externally individuated features. That occurrent thoughts have externally individuated features is accepted also by those who acknowledge both narrow and broad contents (as long as content features are regarded as mental features). Disjunctivists (of any variety) claim that perceptual experiences, which are part of the stream of consciousness, have externally individuated mental features. All commonly held forms of externalism question internalism even in the restricted version I am willing to assert here. Next I shall argue that they are wrong.

6

EXTERNALISM AND PRIVILEGED SELF-KNOWLEDGE

6.1 Incompatibility and the Usual Understanding

In this chapter I shall join the debate about the compatibility of externalism and privileged self-knowledge. In the first part of this book, I argued that privileged accessibility is the mark of the mental. In this chapter, I shall try to show that externalism poses a limitation on privileged access to our mental features in a way that internalism does not. This is a good argument against externalism.

There has been a lot of back and forth on the question of whether externalism is compatible with privileged self-knowledge, and, though in my final conclusion I side with the incompatibilists, I do not think that all arguments for this side were equally successful. I shall comment on some less successful arguments below.

The first point I would like to make is that the usual understanding of externalism, which draws the boundary between the internal and the external around the skin (or the brain), is liable to obscure the question of the incompatibility of externalism and privileged self-knowledge. At least according to one line of thought, on the usual understanding of externalism, we can expect no significant difference between externalism and materialist internalism in relation to self-knowledge.

Suppose that we accept the usual understanding; then the main difference between a *materialist* internalist and externalist is about where to locate facts on which the content of our mental states depend:

externalism:
    being in a mental state with content *C*
        depends on/entails that
    E (some fact which is outside the body or the brain of the subject)

internalism:
    being in a mental state with content *C*
        depends on/entails that
    B (some fact about the body or the brain)

One can try to articulate the idea that externalism is incompatible with privileged access by contrasting our epistemic status with respect to the first and the second item in the externalist thesis. Thus we know in some special way (directly or a priori or with first-person authority or something like that) that we are in mental state with content *C*, but we do not know in that special way that *E* obtains. And how could something that we know in that special way depend on or entail something we do not know in that special way? The details of the argument are filled in according to what we take to be the 'special way', and according to what we take to be the nature of 'dependence' or 'entailment' between the first and second item. Witness Burge's formulation of the problem in his influential article defending the compatibility thesis:

> Our problem is that of understanding how we can know some of our mental events in a direct, nonempirical manner, when those events depend for their identities on our relations to the environment. A person need not investigate the environment to know what his thoughts are. A person does have to investigate the environment to know what his environment is like. Does this not indicate that mental events are what they are independently of the environment? (Burge 1988: 650)

But, if this is indeed the source of concern about compatibility, then the materialist internalist has as much reason to worry as the externalist has. Consider the formulation of internalism above: the same contrast can be drawn between our epistemic status with respect to the first and second item in the thesis. We certainly do not know directly and non-empirically our brain states, nor, under a similar description, the bodily states that are meant to individuate our mental states. We find out many things about our body in the same way we find out things about our environment: empirically and from the third-person point of view—with the help of X-rays, surgery, or tissue samples.

If the worry formulated above is legitimate, certain versions of dualist internalism might indeed have an advantage over other theories. If being in a mental state does not depend on being in a physical state, then the nature of mental features realized in an immaterial substance is perhaps exhausted by their mental description. There would not be further conditions that are necessary for the mental features to be exemplified, and hence there would not be conditions that are not specially accessible and yet individuate mental features. However, an internalist does not *have* to be a dualist—I, for one, would like to remain neutral on this issue. But then the *only and decisive* difference between internalism and externalism is whether they place facts that individuate mental content within or outside the confines of the body; and, in this case, so far it seems that there is no reason to think that this will result in any interesting epistemological difference between the two theses.

A different and widely discussed attempt to demonstrate the incompatibility of externalism and privileged self-knowledge was formulated by Michael McKinsey (1991: 16): 'if you could know a priori that you are in a given mental state, and your being in that state conceptually or logically implies the existence of external objects, then you could know a priori that the external world exists. Since you obviously don't know a priori that the external world exists, you also can't know a priori that you are in the mental state in question. It's that simple.' I have already indicated my reservations about classifying introspection as a variety of a priori knowledge, if the paradigm of a priori knowledge is knowledge of logic and mathematics. Susana Nuccetelli (1999) has argued convincingly that there is no uniform interpretation of 'a priori' that would figure in both premises of the argument. She further argues that a disjunctive conception of non-empirical—either introspective or a priori—knowledge would cause problems for the inferences employed in the argument. Finally, she claims that we need mixed knowledge, which uses empirical background information, to arrive at the conclusion, and this mixed knowledge can be plausibly regarded as the source of the claim that the external world exists.

6.2 Internalism and Privileged Access

The key to understanding the issue of externalism and privileged self-knowledge is the realization of the connection between privileged self-knowledge and phenomenal properties. It is important to be clear about the features of privileged access that generate its incompatibility with externalism. For the reasons already given (in Section 1.6), I do not think that characterizing introspective self-knowledge as a priori is helpful. Nor do I think that introspection is omniscient or infallible. The crucial feature is privileged access: that what I get to know through introspection is knowable only for me in this way.

In Section 1.6, I said that an explanation of privileged accessibility is offered by the hypothesis that mental facts are perspectival facts; that is, their identity is essentially determined by their being in a way *for* the subject. Facts involving phenomenal properties of sensory experiences—that is, facts about how things look or taste or feel to us—are paradigmatic examples of perspectival facts, since an appearance and a feeling is always *for* a subject, and hence assumes a certain point of view. Nothing could appear or feel in a way without appearing or feeling for someone. When we extended the notion of phenomenal properties to other conscious states or events, this was done through an appeal to their what-it-is-like character. The fundamental logic of 'what-it-is-like' features is the same as the logic of appearances: a what-it-is-like feature is always something it is like for someone, and hence assumes a point of view.

The phenomenal nature of conscious mental events is accessible in a privileged way. According to the internalist position I defend, this exhausts the mental nature of these events. Externalists say that, beyond these perspectival properties, there are further factors that contribute to the mental nature of conscious events. This must mean that, in the externalist view, there are mental properties that are not accessible in a privileged way, because their presence or absence cannot be registered among the facts that are accessible in a privileged way. Externalism poses a limitation on privileged access in a way internalism does not.

The crucial statements of this account are:

1. All and only phenomenal properties of conscious events give rise to perspectival facts.
2. The realm of perspectival facts is the same as the realm that is open to privileged access.
3. Phenomenal properties (properties which are responsible for perspectival facts) are shared by subjects in Twin situations.

Someone who is externalist about phenomenology may feel a resistance to this account. They may agree that phenomenal facts are perspectival facts, but protest that Twins have different phenomenology. I have tried to show that such an account faces a serious problem, since it cannot explain what makes two situations subjectively indistinguishable. The best option for theories with an externalist phenomenology seemed to be to explain subjective indistinguishability in epistemic terms, but this proved to be problematic on various interpretations of the epistemic indiscriminability relation. However, suppose for a moment that I am wrong about this, and there is an analysis of the notion of indiscriminability that is suitable for these purposes. Still, surely the only plausible way to develop such an account is to say that the two situations are *introspectively* (or subjectively) indiscriminable, since there is no reason to think that the situations would not be discriminable through other means—for example, through empirical investigation of the environment or by relying on testimony. So, even on this account, externalism would pose a limitation on introspective knowledge that is not posed by internalism.

In my account, the introspective indiscriminability of Twin situations is explained by two circumstances. First, the phenomenal properties of Twin experiences are the same, and, since everything is indiscriminable from itself—on any notion of indiscriminability—the phenomenal character of the Twins' experiences are indiscriminable; or, in other words, these experiences are indiscriminable with respect to their phenomenal character. Secondly, phenomenal properties, being constitutive of perspectival facts, are precisely the properties knowable through introspection. To use an analogy that I mentioned before, if two things agree in their observable properties, then they cannot be discriminated through observation. Externalists about phenomenology offer the introspective indiscriminability of Twin experiences as a brute fact, and I offer an explanation in terms of their shared phenomenal properties. Nonetheless, the upshot is an agreement over their introspective indiscriminability.

Earlier, I have considered cases where privileged access to my mental states faces an obstacle—for example, in the case of self-deception. I have explained (in Section 2.3) how I suggest to square this with my thesis that the realm of the mental is the realm accessible in a privileged way. There may be similar phenomena in cases of difficulties of grasping complex ideas, or cases of strong emotional involvement. The striking feature of externalism is that it forces a limitation on privileged access that is fundamentally different in character: it arises with respect to the simplest occurrent thoughts and experiences, and it is not explainable by these familiar facts of human psychology. Our introspective cognitive faculty is fallible, and in the familiar problematic cases it stumbles. But, with respect to the allegedly externally individuated mental facts concerning conscious events, it is powerless. Vision is a fallible capacity: when my eyes are tired, I may see only the blurred outlines of an object. However, vision is not simply fallible, but powerless, with respect to invisible properties. And facts that lie outside the subject's point of view are 'invisible' to introspection. Of course, externalism does not completely 'blind' introspection, since I presume that no externalist would want to deny that being in a certain conscious mental state involves also internal facts about the subject—and the internal facts may be accessible in a privileged way. The claim is merely that there will be *some* mental features that lie outside the scope of privileged self-knowledge.

I believe that the above considerations do show that externalism limits privileged self-knowledge, but, since there has been a considerable debate about this issue, and whole books have been published on the subject, I shall probably have to say a bit more to convince. One question that has received a lot of attention is the issue of introspective knowledge of our thoughts and our ability to discriminate them. It has been claimed that, even though there may be a problem with our ability to discriminate certain thoughts if externalism is true, this does not threaten our introspective knowledge. It has also been held that there is an account of privileged self-knowledge that is independent of the outcome of the externalism/internalism debate. I shall take up these points and others in the next sections.

6.3 Contextually Self-Verifying Thoughts

Before I start elaborating my argument for the incompatibility of externalism and privileged self-knowledge, I would like to criticize an argument for the *compatibility* of the two theses. There is a positive account of self-knowledge that is defended, among others, by John Heil (1988) and Tyler Burge (1988, 1996), and that makes the possibility of privileged access independent of the outcome of the internalism/externalism debate, and also independent of whether we define externalism in the usual way or not. The essence of the theory is that second-order thoughts like 'Now I am thinking that water is wet' are contextually self-verifying: since the content of the second-order thought inherits the content of the first-order thought 'water is wet', there is no possibility of mismatch between the two contents. Whether one is on Earth or Twin Earth, one always expresses a *true* thought by 'I am thinking that water is wet', since one inevitably thinks the first-order thought 'water is wet' while thinking the second-order thought that embeds the first-order thought.

The supposedly attractive features of this theory are that (i) it is independent of the internalism/externalism debate, (ii) it accounts for the privileged nature of self-knowledge, since the subject can produce this kind of contextually self-verifying thoughts only concerning her own thoughts, and (iii) it accounts for the non-empirical nature of self-knowledge. Moreover, it chimes with the traditionally held idea that introspection is infallible. If this account is right, then there is no problem about the compatibility of externalism and self-knowledge, since the account is clearly compatible with externalism.

There are two problems with this account. First, as it has been pointed out several times, if the source of knowledge is the contextually-self-verifying character, then introspective knowledge seems analogous to my knowledge of the fact that *I am here*. I cannot go wrong in thinking that I am here, for, wherever that thought is thought, I am always there. But it is clear that knowing that I am here in this way is compatible with not having any idea where I am. It is arguable that in the case of self-knowledge we have this type of more substantial knowledge—and therefore Burge's and Heil's theory does not account for the entire content of self-knowledge. (For more arguments for why the self-ascription of thoughts in this way does not necessarily provide knowledge, see Goldberg 2000.)

The second problem is already anticipated by the discussion of the difference between introspective knowledge and knowledge of contextually self-verifying statements in Section 1.6 (similar consideration were put forward in Boghossian 1989). Burge's and Heil's account of introspective knowledge of thought contents cannot be integrated within a unified account of introspective knowledge of other mental features. One's conscious mental life, the stream of one's consciousness, is characterized by all sorts of phenomenal features in the broad sense canvassed in Chapter 4: feeling slightly hungry, a strong determination to finish a paper on deadline, a mental effort to solve a particular problem, an unexpected memory of a town visited some years ago, the sudden idea of a new line of argument, and so on. These features are all in the scope of introspective knowledge, and introspective knowledge in general is supposed to be non-empirical and privileged. Indeed, the privileged nature of introspection is often illustrated by the way we know our sensory states—that one feels pain, or one has a red visual experience. But most of our judgements about our mental features are not contextually self-verifying. 'I am in pain', and 'I have a visual experience of red', are not true every time they are thought; I have just thought them, and they were false. So whatever accounts for the privileged and non-empirical nature of my knowledge of *these* kind of mental features, it cannot be what is offered by Burge's and Heil's account.

On my own approach, we have a fallible faculty of introspection that allows the subject to learn about all features of her mind, and in a way no one else can. The privileged and non-empirical nature of this kind of knowledge is integral to this faculty, and hence characterizes knowledge of all mental features. In the next section, I shall look further into the question of introspecting various mental features.

6.4 Externalism About Various Mental Features

The most widely held form of externalism about the mental, and the focus of most discussions about externalism and self-knowledge, is externalism about mental *content*. As I have mentioned earlier, externalism can be held about other mental features, and it is instructive to consider the compatibility of these forms of externalism with privileged self-knowledge.

Timothy Williamson (1995, 2000) argued for a version of externalism about *propositional attitudes*. In his view, *knowing* is a state of mind different from merely believing. This contrasts with the more widely held view that knowing that *p* is a state that *includes mental components*: one mental component is the belief that *p*, and there could be some further mental components that amount to the justification of the belief that *p*, depending on one's theory of justification. On this view, there could be two subjects that agree in all mental respects—in the belief component, and even in the justification components—and yet one of them has knowledge, while the other does not. This is not possible, according to Williamson, since whether one knows something or not is itself a feature of one's mind.

Williamson's view is a form of externalism about the mental, since internally identical subjects can differ in their knowledge properties. Consider one of Williamson's examples, someone who knows that Lincoln is the President of the United States. Her knowledge ceases at the moment when Lincoln is shot, but this may not involve any internal change in her. Or we may assume that in a counterfactual situation Lincoln is shot ten minutes before the time he is shot in the actual situation; then the actual subject and her counterfactual counterpart may be in exactly the same internal state, and yet one knows that Lincoln is President, the other does not. In Williamson's view, this means that their mental states are different in the two situations, despite internal sameness, so we have a form of externalism about the mental.

In this case, it is an acknowledged consequence of the externality of the mental feature that the subject is not in the position to know merely by reflection that the feature is present or absent. Williamson considers this as a possible objection to regarding knowing as a mental feature, the objection being that mental features should be reflectively accessible, but he thinks the objection is not well founded.

Disjunctivism about perceptual experiences is also a form of externalism about mental features. In fact, Williamson's view can be regarded as a version of disjunctivism, since he would hold that a veridical perception and a corresponding hallucination belong to different fundamental mental kinds, one being a case of knowledge and the other not. Other disjunctivists may not share Williamson's view about knowledge in general, but would have a disjunctive view specifically about perceptual experience. In the earlier discussion, I distinguished a more moderate form of disjunctivism, which acknowledges a shared phenomenal character between experiences—this would, for example, as I understand it, be Williamson's position—and a version that denies any common factor between a VP and a corresponding H. In either version of disjunctivism, internally identical subjects could be in different mental states because one perceives and the other hallucinates (Martin 2004).

Here again, it is generally acknowledged that the absence or presence of the externally constituted mental feature cannot be known through reflection. In fact, for at least one prominent disjunctivist, M. G. F. Martin, it is a key feature of the account that, when one is hallucinating, one cannot know, by reflection, that one is hallucinating, that is, that one is not having a veridical perception. A further question is whether the account is also committed to saying that when one is having a veridical perception, one cannot know through reflection that one is in such a state. There are good reasons to think that the answer to this question is positive (see Section 5.8 about mutual indiscriminability).

This does not mean that the epistemic situations of veridical perceiving and hallucinating are symmetrical. As it happens, I believe that I can know that I am not hallucinating on some occasions, like the present one: since I know I am typing on a computer, and I know that typing on a computer entails that I am not hallucinating, and since knowledge is deductively closed, I know that I am not hallucinating. But I know the first premise, that I am typing on a computer *empirically*, and hence my knowledge that I am not hallucinating is not all coming from introspection. If I relied merely on introspection, I could not know that I was not hallucinating.

In contrast, if I were hallucinating, I would lack the kind of empirical knowledge that served as a starting point for my argument in the perceptual state, so in that case there would be occasions when I did not know at all that I was hallucinating. As a previous example showed, it is not altogether impossible to know that one is hallucinating; a combination of testimony and memory could do the trick. However, the point is that one cannot know merely through reflection that one is having a veridical perception, or that one is having a hallucination. Consequently, on the views that make these features constitutive of different mental states, the reflective access to one's mental features is limited.

Now consider a different kind of example. On the so-called social-externalist view, defended by Tyler Burge, among others, the use of words in the subject's linguistic community can be an external factor in determining the content of the subject's thoughts. Internally identical subjects who are placed in different linguistic communities can therefore have different thoughts. Suppose that, in a counterfactual linguistic community, the community's use of the words 'nausea' and 'vertigo' are swapped compared to the actual situation. Consider actual world Alfred and his counterfactual internal duplicate, Twin Alfred. Since they are internal duplicates, both would say that nausea is the sensation of discomfort in the stomach, with an urge to vomit, and vertigo is the sensation of spinning and swaying. Nonetheless, according to social externalists, they express different thoughts when they say 'I have nausea' or 'I have vertigo', because the content of these thoughts is determined by the use of the terms in their community.

Suppose Alfred believes that he has nausea and he does not have vertigo; according to social externalism, the content of Twin Alfred's parallel belief that he would express using the same words is that he has vertigo, and not nausea. They both have a sensation of discomfort in the stomach but not of spinning, so, on the social-externalist view, Alfred is right and Twin Alfred is wrong. This case is analogous to Burge's arthritis case (1979), where both Alf and his counterfactual internal duplicate believe that they have arthritis in the thigh, but, while Alf is wrong, his counterpart is right. The difference in the present case is that we have a word denoting a sensation rather than an ailment (and the actual subject is right and the counterfactual subject is wrong).

6.5 Failure of Privileged Access

We have seen three cases where it was claimed that some statement concerning one's mental features have externally individuated truth conditions:

1. 'I know that I am typing on a computer.'
2. 'I veridically perceive that I am typing on a computer.'
3. 'I am having nausea.'

In the first two cases, it would probably be generally agreed that the truth conditions are externally individuated; the controversial thesis is that they state purely mental features (rather than features with a mental component). In the third case, I expect a general agreement that the statement attributes mental features; the question is whether the truth conditions are really externally individuated.

In any case, three points should be noted about these three statements. First, it is possible to entertain all three thoughts expressed by these sentences while the thoughts are false. If you are reading this book, it is likely that you have just done so. Secondly, in the first two cases, there are circumstances when one can have a false *belief* expressed by these statements (beyond merely entertaining the thought), and, if content externalism is true, then, in the situation described above, a subject has a false belief concerning his sensations—that is, has a false belief expressed by the third sentence. Thirdly, in these cases the subjects fail to have privileged access to their mental features, and this clearly has to do with the externality of the feature. It is because of the possibility of subjectively indistinguishable situations where one knows or does not know, or perceives or merely hallucinates, that one cannot tell, merely by reflection, that one is hallucinating, or that one is veridically perceiving.

One may be tempted to say that, in the third case, the subject possesses the requisite self-knowledge, because he can identify introspectively the sensation; the problem is only that the statement he utters is false because its content is externally determined. In some sense, I think this is right, since I think the overwhelmingly plausible analysis of that case is that Twin Alfred has the same thoughts concerning his *sensations* as Alfred has, and these are correct, and the only thing that is wrong with him is that he mistakenly thinks that nausea is called 'vertigo' (see Crane 1991 for this analysis of the Burge cases). But social externalists deny this; they are committed to the claim that Twin Alfred has false beliefs concerning his sensations, beliefs he expresses as 'I have nausea, I do not have vertigo'. Would the situation be different if he did not use the words 'nausea' and 'vertigo'? Suppose he said: 'I am having *this* sensation.' That statement would be right, but so would be the hallucinating subject's claim that 'I am having *this kind* of experience'. It would still be true that the introspective knowledge of the subject has a certain defect.

If a mental feature is individuated externally, the truth conditions of the statement by which the subject attributes to herself the feature are external to the subject. Attributing a mental feature to herself involves the subject's thinking that she has the feature. We saw some cases where *thinking* that one has a mental feature does not imply that one *has* the mental feature, and where the externality of the feature implied a deficiency in the subject's introspective knowledge of the feature. Now the most commonly investigated cases in the debate about the compatibility of externalism and self-knowledge are cases of knowing the content of one's thoughts. These cases are quite special, because, as we saw in the previous sections, self-attribution of a content creates a self-verifying statement. When one thinks that one thinks a thought, then one is guaranteed to be correct. But, as we also saw, guaranteed correctness is not sufficient for knowledge. Even though I am always right in thinking that I am here, this is compatible with not having any idea where I am. Even though I am always right in thinking that I have the type of experience I have, this is compatible with my lack of introspective knowledge of whether I am veridically perceiving or hallucinating.

Let me reiterate the point I made in Section 6.3 about the unity of the introspective faculty. We have privileged access to the features of our conscious mental events, including their sensory, cognitive, and conative aspects. An account that grants privileged access only to some of these, but not to all, is incomplete. There is general reason to think that externalism limits the scope of privileged access, and this is quite clear in cases where the externality touches a mental feature other than the content of a thought. In the case of self-attribution of contents, the deficiency in knowledge created by externalism is obscured by the fact that the self-attribution creates a self-verifying statement. But the self-verifying nature is not sufficient to account for privileged self-knowledge, because (i) guaranteed correctness is not sufficient for knowledge, and (ii) the self-verifying nature cannot be the basis of a general account of privileged self-knowledge, since it does not apply to all mental features that we can access in a privileged way.

6.6 Travelling Cases

I have been arguing that the main reason for thinking that externalism is in conflict with privileged access is that, according to externalists, I could be in a situation that was subjectively indiscriminable from my present situation, where some of my mental features were different. As we saw, this latter claim should be granted even by those who are externalist about phenomenology, if they want to have some account of the Twin situations.

Privileged access reaches only what falls within the subject's point of view; if the presence or absence of a feature cannot be registered subjectively, we do not have privileged access to the feature in question.

This argument apparently follows a line of reasoning that has been used to support the incompatibility of externalism and self-knowledge in a number of forms (and has also received extensive criticism). According to this line of reasoning, externalism has the consequence that, in some cases, we cannot introspectively *discriminate* between different thought contents, and, according to a further consideration, this shows that our introspective knowledge of these contents is deficient.

The argument is often supported by the so-called travelling cases. Oscar spends the first part of his life on Earth, and one night he is unwittingly transported to Twin Earth; better even, he is swapped with Twin Oscar. Since everything looks the same on Twin Earth, he does not notice the change, and he goes on with his life (or rather his Twin's life). Most externalists agree that, if he spends enough time in his new environment, the concept he expresses by the word 'water' switches to express *twater* rather than *water*; or perhaps it becomes a mixed concept including both water and twater in its extension. In any case, the concept changes. It is part of the externalist view that this change need not be accompanied by any internal change that is registered by Oscar.

Suppose Oscar is thinking a thought he would express as 'water is wet'. It is said that he cannot discriminate by reflection the content of this thought from the alternative content he would have had, had he remained on Earth and continued to have his old water concept. It is true that his second-order thoughts like 'I am now thinking that water is wet' remain correct, since the content of the second-order thought switches together with the content of the first-order thought. However, the further suggestion is that, since he cannot discriminate his present twater-thinking situation from the relevant alternative of a water-thinking situation, he does not know that he is now thinking of twater. Once the possibility of travel is made relevant, the point extends to all broad contents; even before Oscar was transported to Twin Earth, he could not discriminate his water thoughts from the counterfactual twater thoughts he would have had if he had been transported to Twin Earth at some time prior to that.

Travelling cases are supposed to show that we cannot introspectively discriminate thought contents, and that this affects introspective knowledge of content. Critics of this argument try to show either that, contrary to first impressions, we can discriminate between the contents in question (McLaughlin and Tye 1998); or that failure of discriminatory knowledge is not detrimental to knowledge *simpliciter* (Falvey and Owens 1994). I shall look at the details of these suggestions in the next sections.

Some progress can hopefully be made on this issue if we try to clarify in what sense discrimination is supposed to be necessary for knowledge. After all, in a certain sense, all cases of ignorance can be described as failures of discrimination: if someone did not know that her shoelaces were undone, we could say that she could not discriminate her present situation from the situation where her shoelaces are not undone. The notion of indiscriminability involved here is access indiscriminability: if S knows that *p*, then her present situation is access discriminable from situations where *p* is false. This is not very illuminating though, because the condition follows simply from the definition of access indiscriminability. If we want a more substantial necessary condition for knowledge, and if we want to evaluate its plausibility, we need a more precise idea of what discrimination involves when it is claimed to be necessary for knowledge.

6.7 Discrimination and Introspective Knowledge

When the claim that discrimination is necessary for knowledge is used in an argument about travelling cases, the reference is often to the work of Alvin Goldman, who defends the view that discrimination is necessary for perceptual knowledge. As Goldman (1976: 774) puts it: 'A person knows that *p*, I suggest, only if the actual state of affairs in which *p* is true is *distinguishable* or *discriminable* by him from a relevant possible states of affairs in which *p* is false.'

It is fairly clear that Goldman himself interprets the kind of discriminability that he regards as necessary for perceptual knowledge as *response* discriminability in the sense introduced in Section 5.9 (he does not use this terminology). As I remarked earlier, this notion does not make use of the concept of knowledge, and hence it is especially suitable for providing a non-circular necessary condition for perceptual knowledge. Response discriminability is definable in naturalistic terms—in terms of responses to certain stimuli—and this fits well Goldman's reliabilist conception of justification. There is a straightforward connection between the reliability and the discriminative powers of a cognitive mechanism: 'To be reliable, a cognitive mechanism must enable a person to *discriminate* or *differentiate* between incompatible states of affairs. It must operate in such a way that incompatible states of the world would generate different cognitive responses' (Goldman 1976: 771).

This is a clear statement of the response discriminability requirement. One example Goldman uses to illustrate the claim that discrimination is necessary for perceptual knowledge is the—by now very familiar—example of Henry, who sees a barn from the road when travelling in the countryside, and forms the belief that there is a barn there. But, unbeknownst to Henry, the country in question has a lot of fake barns, made of papier mâché, which nonetheless look like real barns from a certain distance. In this case, we are inclined to say that Henry has no knowledge that what he sees is a barn, and Goldman explains this inclination by the fact that Henry cannot discriminate his present situation from the one where he sees a fake barn: 'Since, by assumption, a state of affairs in which such a hypothesis holds is indistinguishable by Henry from the actual state of affairs (from his vantage point on the road), this hypothesis is not "ruled out" or "precluded" by the factors that prompt Henry's belief' (Goldman 1976: 774–5).

So Goldman is committed to the following claims about perceptual knowledge and Henry's particular case:

1. Discrimination is necessary for perceptual knowledge.
2. Henry cannot discriminate his current situation of facing a real barn from the relevant counterfactual situation of facing a fake barn.
3. Therefore Henry does not know that he is facing a real barn.

People have been debating whether the travelling case is a basis for a similar argument. To decide this, we need to consider whether the following claims are true:

(I) The discrimination requirement extends to introspective knowledge.

(II) Travelling Oscar's situation is similar to that of Henry in the following respect: he cannot discriminate his present situation of thinking about water from a relevant alternative of thinking about twater.

(III) Therefore Oscar does not know that he is thinking of water.

Accepting both (I) and (II) and concluding (III) is the classic version of the travelling argument for the incompatibility of externalism and privileged introspective knowledge.

But, if Goldman's account is the model to follow when we set up the connection between discrimination and knowledge, then the relevant notion is response discriminability, and then the water-thinking and twater-thinking situations are apparently *discriminable*. As we have already seen, different first-order thoughts generate different second-order thoughts—that is, different cognitive responses. If this is right, then the travelling subject's case is *not* analogous to Henry's case with the fake barns (that is, (II) in the travelling argument does not obtain). Then one can adopt externalism about content, extend the requirement of discriminability to introspective knowledge—that is, accept (I)—and uphold the view that we have introspective knowledge of our thoughts (reject (III)). On this interpretation, the travelling argument does not show the incompatibility of externalism and privileged self-knowledge.

6.8 Access Discriminability and Introspective Knowledge

A different response to the travelling argument is given by Kevin Falvey and Joseph Owens, who apparently accept a version of (II), the analogy between Henry's case and the travelling cases, but reject (I), the extension of the discrimination requirement to introspection, and choose to resist (III) in this way (although they use different conceptual apparatus, so there is another way of constructing their position).

Falvey and Owens (1994: 116) formulate a Relevant Alternatives principle operative in Henry's case as follows:

(RA) If (i) *q* is a relevant alternative to *p*, and (ii) S's belief that *p* is based on evidence that is compatible with its being the case that *q*, then S does not know that *p*.

If we translate this into a necessary condition for knowledge that *p*, we get the following (for every *q* that is a relevant alternative to *p*):

(RA2) S's belief that *p* is not based on evidence that is compatible with its being the case that *q*.

The notion involved here is a variation on the access conception of discriminability, between one's present situation and a situation where *q* is true (which I shall call the '*q*-situation'). The difference compared to the version discussed before is that the requirement of discriminability is not that 'for all the subject *knows*, she could not be in the *q*-situation', but rather 'for all the subject *has evidence for*, she could not be in the *q*-situation'. It is worth pointing out that, if we adopt Timothy Williamson's—to my mind, very plausible—view that knowledge is evidence (Williamson 2000), these two statements are equivalent.[1]

Falvey and Owens hold that the travelling subject's (theirs is called 'Susan') belief concerning her water thoughts is based on evidence that is *compatible* with the twater-thinking alternative, and hence that the discriminability condition embodied in (RA) does not hold: 'Susan cannot point to evidence in her experiential history that rules out the hypothesis that she is on Twin-Earth thinking that twater is liquid. Such a situation would be evidentially indistinguishable from her actual situation' (Falvey and Owens 1994: 117). However, they think that (RA) is not valid for introspective knowledge, because they hold that Susan does know she is thinking of water. The explanation of why Susan has knowledge is familiar: because, unlike Henry in the barn case, she is not liable to form false beliefs about her thought contents. So, even though both Susan and Henry base their belief on evidence that is compatible with a relevant alternative, her immunity and his proneness to error explain why she is knowledgeable, while he is ignorant. So Falvey and Owens endorse (II)—the analogy between Henry's case and the travelling case, as far as the ability to discriminate is concerned—but, since they reject (I), they can resist the conclusion of (III).

One may wonder, though, whether this is a coherent position. If the evidential situations were the same, is it not odd that one subject has knowledge, and the other does not? Indeed, Brian McLaughlin and Michael Tye (1998) argue that Falvey and Owens's claim that

[1] There is a certain complication introduced here by the idea that the evidence under consideration is specifically evidence that the subject's belief is *based on*. We can see the motivation for introducing this qualification: if S had evidence (or knowledge) that was incompatible with his being in a *q*-situation, but this evidence did not play any role in his forming the belief that *p*, then we may want to deny that S knows *p*. However, a whole new issue is opened if we ask whether all knowledge has to be based on *some* evidence. The necessary condition can be satisfied either if the belief is based on incompatible evidence, or if it's not based on any evidence. I'm going to ignore this point, because I don't think it makes much difference to the present issue.

Susan's introspective evidence would be the same in the actual and the alternative situation is based on an unnecessarily restrictive notion of evidence. In fact, we could regard the very thoughts we access directly as pieces of introspective evidence, and in that case Susan *does* have evidence that rules out the possibility that she is thinking about twater. We can still accept (I) and extend the discrimination requirement to introspection, because, if (II) is rejected, (III) does not need to be endorsed.

One thing that may cause some confusion here is running together the different notions of discrimination. The (RA) principle is essentially in terms of the *access* understanding: the subject's evidence is incompatible with the relevant alternative. As we saw, the access conception does not require that the subject can activate knowledge that her situation is distinct from an alternative, for some presentation of the alternative situation; the subject may not even form any idea of the alternative situation (as most of us would not have any notion of travelling alternatives). But, when Falvey and Owens say that Susan *cannot point to evidence* that rules out the alternative hypothesis, this sounds like a deficiency in her knowledge concerning the distinctness of her present and the alternative situation. In other words, it sounds like a deficiency in her *active* discriminatory capacities. But this would not prevent Susan from satisfying the access discriminability condition embodied in (RA), unless we require that, whenever one has evidence, one can point to that evidence. In Section 6.10 below, I shall look at another condition that Falvey and Owens formulate that is clearly in terms of active discriminability, and hence different from (RA).

6.9 Discrimination Through Externally Individuated Contents

It seems that the analysis of the travelling cases so far has not offered support for the incompatibilist position. Discrimination as a necessary condition for knowledge is most plausibly formulated by using either the response or the access notion of discriminability. But as we have seen already in Sections 5.7 and 5.8, if externalism is true, then water thoughts are apparently introspectively discriminable from twater thoughts both in the response and in the access sense. Therefore, it seems that one cannot argue on the analogy of, say, the barn case that we do not have introspective knowledge of broad contents, because a necessary condition of discriminability is not met.

This, however, is only one part of the story. Another part is that Goldman's model of discrimination as a necessary condition for knowledge becomes pointless, *even for perceptual knowledge*, once contents are externally individuated. Consider one of Goldman's examples, identical twins Judy and Trudy. On a widely accepted externalist view of content, the content of someone's belief expressed as 'She is standing right in front of me' is different, depending on whether it is Judy, or Trudy, who is standing in front of him. (The externalist view contrasts with my own internalist theory, on which the content of 'She is standing in front of me' remains the same as long as the accompanying phenomenal states are the same. I defend the viability of this view in Chapter 7.) On some externalist theories, the contents of the corresponding perceptual states are going to be different, too. So at least some of this person's cognitive responses to Judy's presence and Trudy's presence are different: he responds to their respective presence with different beliefs. But this is true of a person who, for all intents and purposes, cannot tell Judy and Trudy apart, and therefore *does not know* which of them he is facing.

The point here is not that the subject's thoughts about Judy and Trudy are different, and therefore his second-order thoughts about his Judy and Trudy thoughts are different—though, of course, this is true too. The present point is that *his first-order cognitive responses* to Judy's and Trudy's presence, the *empirical beliefs* he forms when facing them, are different. So, if discriminability of *A* and *B* requires that the subject gives different cognitive responses to *A* and *B*, then, since in the twins' case this condition is met, the subject is able empirically to discriminate Judy and Trudy. In fact, he will be able to discriminate them infallibly: for, if the content of indexical thoughts is individuated by the referent of the indexical, then the subject's cognitive response always concerns just the right individual. Then the ability to discriminate ceases to be a useful condition to mark cases of empirical knowledge and ignorance: for the onlooker who cannot tell whether he is facing Judy or Trudy will be able to 'discriminate' them (in the present sense of the term) just as reliably as the twins' mother, who, in contrast, can actually tell whether she is facing Judy or Trudy. (The same considerations apply, *mutatis mutandis,* if the notion is access indiscriminability.)

One might say that this result is not counter-intuitive, since the discriminability requirement should surely be put forward as a *necessary*, rather than as a necessary and sufficient, condition for knowledge. Independently of the issue of externalism, mere difference in cognitive responses is not sufficient for knowledge, if the responses are not properly integrated among the subject's other beliefs. So, even if the ignorant onlooker *can* response discriminate Judy from Trudy, we can still explain why he does not know he is facing, say, Judy on a given occasion, because *other conditions* are not met.

However, the ordinary cases where there is a difference in cognitive response and yet there is no knowledge are rather different from the externalist case. For example, it may be the case that Judy has a mole on her face and Trudy does not; one's perceptual experiences when looking at the twins are different, hence the necessary condition of discriminability is met. Even so, if someone does not realize that this is a way to distinguish Judy and Trudy, he still may not know which of them he is facing on a given occasion. But the discrimination resulting from the different content of indexical sentences is rather different. It is not an unused clue that could be conducive of knowledge once one realizes its significance. Even if two things presented exactly the same perceptual appearance—so there were no discoverable perceptual clues to their difference—one would produce different cognitive responses by forming the appropriate indexical sentences. It is unclear how this 'discrimination' could be integrated into, or be made useful for, one's general stock of knowledge. Jessica Brown (2004: 491 ff.) makes a similar point when she describes how discrimination through second-order thoughts with broad content is independent from several other abilities we normally expect to go together with discriminatory abilities, like the abilities to notice change or to act differentially.

The debate has so far been inconclusive. We have not seen a reason to give up the requirement of discriminability as necessary for knowledge, but, if we borrow the notion of discrimination that figures in the most widely accepted formulations of the discriminability requirement for perceptual knowledge, then water and twater thoughts are discriminable. At the same time, the discriminability resulting from externally individuated cognitive responses ceases to be an interesting condition for knowledge. Of course, the discriminability condition was offered as merely necessary and not sufficient, but, even so, in ordinary circumstances, the ability to discriminate points towards at least the possibility of some cognitive achievement. This is apparently not the case with discrimination resulting from broad cognitive responses. In the next section, I shall look at some further interesting lessons offered by the travelling cases.

6.10 The 'Transparency' of Content

Falvey and Owens formulate a principle that they call 'introspective knowledge of *comparative* content': 'With respect to any two of his thoughts or beliefs, an individual can know authoritatively and directly (that is, without relying on inferences from his observed environment) whether or not they have the same content' (Falvey and Owens 1994: 109–10). The claim is also known as the 'transparency of content' claim (Boghossian 1994). Falvey and Owens maintain that the travelling cases show that externalism is not compatible with introspective knowledge of *comparative* content (I shall explain below why). But they think this principle is false anyway, independently of externalism. Furthermore, they also claim that ignorance of comparative content does not threaten 'straight' introspective knowledge of content.

As far as I understand it, Falvey and Owens offer this principle as a condition of discrimination about one's thoughts and beliefs; a condition that could be claimed to be necessary for knowledge—though, of course, not by them, but by the incompatibilists they criticize. But note that the principle contains a requirement of *active discriminability* of thought contents: the subject has to activate knowledge concerning the distinctness (or sameness) of contents. In the discussion so far, we have not seen a well-articulated suggestion to make some form of active indiscriminability a necessary condition for knowledge; the proposed necessary conditions were in terms of response or access discriminability.

Can we formulate a general necessary condition for knowledge in terms of active indiscriminability (in the way it is done, for example, with access indiscriminability in principle (RA) above)? Presumably, such a condition would look something like this: a subject claims knowledge of *p*; some situations where *p* is false are relevant alternatives; and activating knowledge that her current situation is distinct from these relevant alternatives is necessary for knowledge. In this form, the condition is not specific enough, because of the familiar point about the presentation sensitivity of active indiscriminability. To make it plausible, we should find an adequate way of presenting the relevant alternative (assuming that the subject's current situation is presented as 'my current situation'). It is quite clear that requiring discriminability under all presentations is too strong; and requiring discriminability under some presentation (further unspecified) is too weak.

Finding an adequate general formulation of such a condition would take up too much space and would lead far from our present concerns. Instead, I shall ask how plausible the principle is in itself—that is, whether it is reasonable to expect that we can actively introspectively discriminate our concepts and thought contents—independently of the question of whether this is necessary for something else. Then I shall ask how externalism affects this issue.

First—as always when active discriminability is the issue—we have to get clear about the adequate presentations for the contents. The thought I was entertaining a few minutes ago can be presented as 'the thought KF was entertaining at 12.44' or 'the thought KF was entertaining when someone rang the doorbell', and one may wonder whether this thought had the same content as 'the thought KF entertained at 12.14'. When talking about the transparency of content or concepts, we are not interested in comparing thoughts under such presentations. What we are interested in is a subject who entertains contents *p* and *q* (or concepts *F* and *G*) and tries to find out through direct reflection whether they are the same or not.

It is perfectly possible that someone actually fails in such a task. For example, it is possible that someone applies a word in two patterns of use that express different concepts, and does not realize that she is doing so. The phenomenon I have in mind is not simply that the word has two public meanings that she is not aware of; rather, that she herself means something different by the two uses, which is evidenced in the different dispositions and commitments that she attaches to them. An example may be the way some people use the term 'discrimination' and its cognates in the present debate in different senses, without realizing that they are doing so. The phenomenon is known as the fallacy of equivocation, and it is clearly possible, since it is very much actual.

Occasionally we are ignorant about the distinctness of the concepts expressed by our words, especially, as the above example shows, when the concepts are complex. This further supports my view that introspection—like all our cognitive abilities, including reasoning—is fallible. Falvey and Owens have another example involving a very complex meaning, where people debate whether two contents are the same or not. So the crucial point is not the possibility of mistake, but rather the way we can try to avoid those mistakes. Falvey and Owens think that, in their example, people can find out whether the contents in question are the same or not by investigating the use of words in the linguistic community, which is an external matter. I do not see that at all. Of course, if I am interested in the question of how other people use some term, I shall investigate their usage. But, when I am interested in my own meaning, I shall reflect on my own commitments and putative uses. And all this can be reconstructed from the armchair, by imagining situations and asking myself whether I would be willing to use a term. There is no guarantee that the attempt will be successful in every case, but the expectation is that equivocations should be avoidable in this manner, and anyone who fails in this breaches some norm of rationality.

6.11 External Feature Outside the Scope of Privileged Access

Externalism has the consequence that sometimes it is impossible for a subject to avoid equivocation through a proper use of reason and introspection, as the following example by Paul Boghossian (1994, slightly modified here) shows. Suppose that Oscar has undergone switching and his present use of the word 'water' expresses the concept *twater*. Still, there is no reason to assume that the concept that figures in his beliefs about his past Earthly water experiences switches too: when he recalls visiting Lake Baikal some years ago (which in fact took place back on Earth), and says that 'the water in Lake Baikal was incredibly clean', his word refers to Lake Baikal and H_2O. He now visits Twin Lake Baikal, and, after forming the belief that he would express as 'the water in Lake Baikal is incredibly clean', he concludes that 'the quality of the water in Lake Baikal has not changed'. This inference is mistaken, because it involves equivocation on the words 'water' and 'Lake Baikal'. Everyone would of course agree that he is making some kind of mistake. But the internalist can plausibly say that the the mistake is *factual*: since Oscar mistakenly believes that Lake Baikal and Twin Lake

Baikal are the same, and water and twater are the same substance, he applies same concept to them, respectively. In contrast, the externalist is committed to saying that the mistake is *logical*. Yet no amount of reflection will help Oscar to realize his logical mistake.

In this situation, Oscar directly compares two contents (or two concepts) that he presently grasps. Unlike in the earlier considerations, where response or access discriminability was the issue, the comparison here is *not* between concepts entertained in the actual situation and some counterfactual or past situation; instead, both concepts are actually 'before his mind'.

In an important respect, this scenario is different from the temporal phenomenal sorites discussed in Section 5.6. Temporal phenomenal sorites series are created when one is going through a series of sensory experiences that are phenomenally slightly different. The comparison cannot be direct, that is, the situation is set up in a way that one does not have—often cannot have—the two different phenomenal characters simultaneously exemplified in one's conscious experience. In order to activate knowledge that the phenomenal character of one's present sensory experience is different from that of the previous experience, one has to rely on memory; but memory cannot preserve the exact details of phenomenal characters once they have left the subject's consciousness. The situation is different with concepts expressed by words like 'water' or 'Lake Baikal'. The concepts employed in Oscar's beliefs about his past and present encounter are both fully available for direct conscious comparison.

But, even though he can directly compare them, if the concepts are externally individuated, Oscar still cannot find out their difference by introspection. The reason is familiar: for their difference is constituted by a feature that has no trace among the phenomenal features of Oscar's conscious mental life. This difference is surely part of the mental nature of these concepts, and yet it is completely hidden from the introspective faculty. So there are some features of one's conscious mental life (in this case, the aspects that constitute a difference in the content of some conscious thoughts one is entertaining) that are not accessible in a privileged way, if externalism is true.

Let me summarize the discussion about discriminability and privileged self-knowledge. We have seen one typical form of the argument for the incompatibility of externalism and self-knowledge: the argument starts with some general necessary condition for knowledge in terms of access or response discriminability, and claims that this condition is not met in the case of the subject of the travelling scenario. But this argument gets nowhere, since discrimination that is due entirely to cognitive responses with externally individuated contents ceases to be an interesting condition for knowledge. So, even though the condition is automatically satisfied, this does not shed much light on the epistemic status of the subject concerning her own thoughts. However, there is a different kind of argument that does show that externalism limits the scope of privileged self-knowledge. When a subject consciously entertains two concepts whose difference is external to her, she cannot detect their difference in a privileged way, precisely because the difference is to be found in a fact that is outside the phenomenal, and hence the specially accessible features of her mental life.

But this result, I claim, is incompatible with our fundamental notion of the mental, which is based on the idea that the mental realm is accessible to the subject in a way it is accessible to no one else, as I tried to show in Part One of this book. In Chapters 1–3 I argued that our notion of what belongs to the mind depends on what is available to us in a privileged manner. Internalism is deeply routed in what we regard as belonging to the mind, and in the ensuing conception of a person who has the kind of mind we have. But then externalism goes against this conception, since the externally individuated features are necessarily beyond the reach of privileged access.

7

REFERENCE AND SENSE

7.1 Phenomenal and Externalistic Intentionality

In Part Two of the book, I have argued that internalism should be understood as the thesis that the introspectively available phenomenal properties of our conscious mental life determine all its mental features, and these of course also include content properties. The content of a mental state or event is its feature that is responsible for its semantic properties—that is, for its reference and satisfaction conditions. These properties are also known as 'intentional' or 'representational' properties. Judgements and assertions are typical intentional states that aim at the truth. When we formulate a judgement or assert a statement, we lay a claim of truth upon the world: the world has to be in a certain state for our endeavour to succeed. Now, even when arguments like the ones I put forward about privileged self-knowledge, and related arguments about rationality and agency, are presented in defence of internalism, it is often claimed that internalism faces a decisive objection: for internally individuated states are not suitable for laying a claim of truth upon the world. There is no proper intentionality that is constituted by internal features alone.

There have been various responses to this charge. I have already mentioned Terence Horgan, John Tienson, and George Graham, and also Brian Loar and Charles Siewert, who defend a conception of phenomenal intentionality that is the mind's phenomenally manifest direction upon features of the world (Horgan and Tienson 2002; Horgan et al. 2004; Siewert 1998; Loar 2003). They argue, very convincingly, that it is part of the phenomenology of many conscious mental states that they appear to present various features of the world; that this is something that would be shared, for example, between my experiences and the experiences of my vat-brain counterpart. From a different set of assumptions, David Chalmers (2002) argued that there is a notion of narrow (that is, internally individuated) content that does indeed deserve the name 'content' because it determines bona fide truth conditions.

I will not repeat these arguments here, but would like to add a further development. The defenders both of phenomenal intentionality and of narrow content hold that, apart from the internally constituted intentional features, there is also another kind of intentionality: 'externalistic' intentionality, in Horgan et al.'s terminology; 'broad' content in the usual vocabulary of dual-content theorists. Chalmers calls his narrow content 'epistemic', and his broad content 'subjunctive' content. Externalist theories are supposed to be right about this other kind of intentionality or content. In the familiar Twin Earth scenario, the thoughts that Oscar and Twin Oscar would both express by saying 'water fills the oceans' have the same narrow content (phenomenal intentional features), but different broad content (externalistic intentional features).

My own internalist theory cannot recognize externally individuated contents, if these are supposed to be mental features, since my view is that all mental features (at least of conscious mental states) are internal. In what follows, I shall defend this view.

7.2 The 'Inexpressibility of Narrow Content'

I said above that the content of a mental state is a feature that is responsible for the state's semantic properties. This characterization, while part of the notion of content I have in mind, is too abstract in itself. In line with the phenomenal determination of our mental features defended in this book, I would also like to say that the content of a thought or a judgement is what we *grasp* when we think the thought, or reflect upon a belief. The episodes in my conscious life are characterized by their psychological features. When I think to myself 'You could not step twice into the same river', there is something I grasp, something that is present to my mind, something that makes this event of thinking different from the event of thinking 'You can very well step twice into the same river'. And that is content.

Frege's notion of 'thought' is a predecessor of our notion of content, since—as we shall see in the next section—'thoughts' are responsible for truth conditions. Frege's term actually reflects well this other feature of contents: that they are grasped in our conscious cogitations. This feature is clearly related to the role that contents are supposed to play in the explanation of actions. Frege describes this as follows:

> How does a thought act? By being apprehended and taken to be true. This is a process in the inner world of a thinker which can have further consequences in this inner world, and which, encroaching on the sphere of the will, can also make itself noticeable in the outer world. If, for example, I grasp the thought which we express by the theorem of Pythagoras, the consequence maybe that I recognize it to be true, and, further, that I apply it, making a decision which brings about the acceleration of masses. Thus our actions are usually prepared by thinking and judgement. (Frege 1918: 104)

The application of the dual-content framework to the theory of content (so understood) is that certain thoughts have *two contents*, which in turn determine two different functions from worlds to truth values. But, given that contents are also grasped, I think this is implausible, on phenomenological grounds. When I think to myself 'I am bored', 'water is a liquid', or 'Descartes was a great philosopher', I have only one thing in my mind, respectively, contrary to the dual theory's claim that I have two things in my mind. I cannot convince myself that these thoughts have two equally psychologically real contents. The same applies to the idea that my mental states have two kinds of intentional features. On the conception of mentality that I have been defending, psychologically real features must have phenomenal presence in my mind—but it does not seem to me at all that my thought expressed as 'water is a liquid' would be directed at two different kinds at the same time.

If one was a dual-content theorist, or a believer in two kinds of intentionality, and had to choose one of the contents to be psychologically real, surely, one would choose the narrow or phenomenally construed content. As Frege said, grasping a thought is a process in the inner world of the thinker. Then one wonders about the status of the other kind of content. Perhaps the other kind of content is not really a mental feature, but a posit that is used, for example, for certain mental-state attributions with others. I have no objection to such a theory, but I would refrain from calling this second kind of feature 'content' or 'intentional feature' in the same sense that applies to the first kind.

I assumed that the one single thought content that you and I grasp when saying 'water is a liquid' is the narrow, or phenomenally construed, content. But, interestingly, in the approach that Horgan et al. promote, narrow content turns out to be inexpressible linguistically. Horgan et al. (2004: 32) tell us that

> insofar as ... narrow truth-conditions are formulable linguistically ..., the formulation will employ only these kinds of vocabulary: (i) logical expressions, (ii) predicative expressions designating properties and relations to which the experiencer can mentally refer non-externalistically, and (iii) certain first-person indexical expressions.

I assume—and assume that Horgan et al. assume—that a thought we would express by using, say, a name is not completely equivalent to any thought expressible with the above resources. This means, however, that the narrow content of a thought we would express by using a name is not formulable linguistically. The narrow truth conditions of such thoughts can be expressed only approximately.

Another promoter of a dual-content theory, Jerry Fodor, also worries about the expressibility of narrow content. The narrow content, to remind us, is what is shared by my water thought and my Twin's twater thought. Now what is this exactly? 'What *is* the thought such that when I have it its truth condition is that H_2O is wet and when my Twin has it its truth condition is such that XYZ is wet? What is the concept *water* such that it denotes H_2O in this world and XYZ in the next?' (Fodor 1987: 49–50). According to Fodor, this question is, in a sense, unanswerable, because

> if you mean by content what can be semantically evaluated, then what my water-thoughts share with Twin 'water'-thoughts *isn't* content. Narrow content is radically inexpressible, because it's only content *potentially*; it's what gets to be content when—and only when—it gets to be anchored. We can't—to put it in a nutshell—*say* what Twin-thoughts have in common. This is because what can be said is ipso facto semantically evaluable; and what Twin thoughts have in common is ipso facto not. (ibid. 50)

Horgan et al. (2004: 313) acknowledge that the narrow truth conditions cannot always be given 'compact, cognitively surveyable, formulations', but they do not think this is a decisive problem for their theory. Neither does Fodor think that this is a serious problem. Perhaps they are right. Nonetheless, it seems to me that it would be a rather disappointing compromise for the defender of narrow content to say that we cannot express narrow contents. If narrow contents are psychologically real, are supposed to be guiding actions, are objects of self-knowledge, are essential for rationality, then how come we cannot express them? Therefore it is worth asking whether this consequence could be avoided; and, in what follows, I shall argue that it can. In order to do this, we have to take a closer look at the question of what it means for something to be semantically evaluable, or aiming at the truth, or laying a claim upon the world. The origin of this whole cluster of problems lies, I believe, in Frege's work.

7.3 Frege on Sense and Reference

In his famous paper 'On Sense and Reference' (1892), Frege introduces the distinction between the sense and the reference of a name. The reference of a name is a definite object, and the sense is 'wherein the mode of presentation is contained'. As for the relation between a sign, its sense, and its reference, Frege (1892: 25) says that 'to the sign there corresponds a definite sense and to that in turn a definite reference'. This idea became known in the tradition influenced by Frege as the doctrine that 'sense determines reference'. Throughout the chapter, I shall understand Frege's doctrine as allowing the possibility of an expression with a sense, but without reference. I regard the 'empty reference' as a special case of reference; when an expression does not have reference, I take it that this fact is determined by its sense. The doctrine has been interpreted in various ways; I shall assume here a minimal understanding of determination. *S* determines *R* will mean simply that there is a determinate *R* belonging to every *S*; in other words, that sameness of *S* implies sameness of *R*, and, consequently, difference in *R* implies a difference in *S*.

The claim that sense determines reference has an elementary appeal. Consider names. We use names to talk about things, so a name should somehow direct speaker and hearer towards an object in the world; how would this be done, if not through what the name expresses, its sense? The claim generalizes even to theories that deny that names have Fregean senses; for, whatever the relevant semantic feature of a name is, it should be reference determining—in the case of direct reference theories, simply by being identical to it. Many philosophers agreed in finding the doctrine compelling, as witnessed by the following quotations from John McDowell and Gregory McCulloch:

> Now it seems plausible that the extension of a word as a speaker uses it should be a function of its meaning; otherwise we lose some links that seem to be simply common sense—not part of some possibly contentious philosophical theory—between what words mean on speakers' lips, what those speakers say when they utter those words, and how things have to be for what they say to be true. (McDowell 1992: 305)

> *Sense determines Meaning*. It is easy to see why one should say this. For to suppose otherwise is to suppose that one could grasp a sense and it still not be settled what one was thinking about. In consequence, one would be able to understand a word like 'Istanbul' yet it still be left open what

one was using the word to talk about. Yet this seems absurd: learning the name is just a way of coming to be able to talk about the city. (McCulloch 1995: 66)

Frege also extended the sense/reference distinction to sentences: the sense of a sentence is a *thought*, and the reference of a sentence is its truth value. A thought, Frege says in a later paper (1918), is that for which the question of truth can arise. The determination between sense and reference is upheld in the case of sentences too: it is not only that thoughts *are* true or false, but also that every thought has a determinate truth value. This is indeed an expression of the idea mentioned in Section 7.1: that thoughts lay a claim of truth upon the world. That sense determines reference means that sense is responsible for semantic features (truth and reference).

How seriously Frege took this doctrine is well illustrated by his treatment of a putative counter-example: the case of thoughts expressed by indexical sentences. Here is the relevant passage:

is the thought changeable or is it timeless? The thought we express by the Pythagorean theorem is surely timeless, eternal, unchangeable. But are there not thoughts which are true today but false in six months time? The thought, for example, that the tree is covered with green leaves, will surely be false in six months time. No, for it is not the same thought at all. The words 'this tree is covered with green leaves' are not sufficient by themselves for the utterance, the time of utterance is involved as well. Without the time-indication this gives we have no complete thought, i.e. no thought at all. But this thought, if it is true, is true not only today or tomorrow but timelessly. (Frege 1918: 103)

We quoted Frege saying that there is a determinate sense belonging to a sign, and a determinate reference belonging to a sense. Since the sign–sense–reference sequence is determinate, there should be a determinate reference belonging to every sign, via the mediation of the sense (or, as a special case, it will lack reference). But no single truth value belongs to the sentence 'this tree is covered with green leaves'; the sentence is sometimes true, sometimes false. The solution Frege offers is to save the determination relation between *sense* and *reference*, by giving up the determination between *sign* and *sense*. The sign 'this tree is covered with green leaves' is not sufficient in itself to express a complete thought, so there is no determinate sense it expresses. The thought becomes complete once we add the time of the utterance; in this way, the same sentence will express different senses on different occasions, and the resulting sense will have a determinate reference.

7.4 Aristotle on Beliefs and Truth Values

Perhaps few would agree these days with Frege that the 'reference' of a sentence is its truth value. Some would also question that the determination of reference must always be mediated by a sense. Nonetheless we find that the view that, if two sentences differ in truth value, they cannot express the same thought, is widely endorsed. Two examples from David Kaplan and John Perry:

> If you and I both say to ourselves,
>
> (B) 'I am getting bored'
>
> have we thought the same thing? We could not have, because what you thought was true while what I thought was false. (Kaplan 1989: 39)

> Let us imagine David Hume, alone in his study, on a particular afternoon in 1775, thinking to himself, 'I wrote the *Treatise*'. Can anyone *else* apprehend the thought he apprehended by this? First note that what he thinks is true. So no one could apprehend the same thought, unless they apprehended a true thought. (Perry 1977: 62)

Contents are reasonably regarded as inheriting the role of Fregean 'thoughts': they are truth evaluable, and they are the objects of mental attitudes. Then we can formulate the Fregean principle as the claim that, if two sentences or beliefs differ in truth value, they have different contents. Furthermore, beliefs are individuated by their contents; different contents indicate different beliefs.

We may think that the Fregean principle is simply intuitively plausible: if my belief is true and yours is false, how could we believe the same? But we should not be so quick. Let us consult a philosopher who wrote long before the Frege-inspired view of contents became widely accepted in philosophy. In the *Categories*, Aristotle claims that only substances can change, and then considers a putative counter-example:

> the same statement seems to be both true or false. Suppose, for example, that the statement that somebody is sitting is true; after he has got up this statement will be false. Similarly with beliefs... [But this is different from the way substances change.] For in the case of substances it is by themselves changing that they are able to receive contraries. For what has become cold instead of hot, dark instead of pale, good instead of bad, has changed... Statements and beliefs, on the other hand, themselves remain completely unchangeable in every way; it is because the *actual thing* changes that the contrary comes to belong to them. *For the statement that somebody is sitting remains the same; it is because of the change in the actual thing that it comes to be true at one time and false at another. Similarly with beliefs.* (*Cat.* 4^a21–4^b2; emphasis added)[1]

Aristotle discusses exactly the same problem we have seen earlier addressed by Frege: the sentence 'He is sitting' is true at some time, and becomes false later. This seems to suggest that the same belief or thought can change from being true to being false. Both Frege and Aristotle find the idea that a thought or belief might undergo genuine change objectionable, but the solution they offer is different. Perhaps we can put the point this way: both Frege and Aristotle agree that the *intrinsic* properties of a belief or thought cannot change—whatever these properties are, they are essential to the thought. Thus no genuine change is possible for thoughts, only, as we might say, a mere Cambridge change. Frege thinks that the truth value is an intrinsic—hence essential—property of a thought, unlike the relational and inessential property of, say, being grasped by me. In contrast, Aristotle thinks that the truth value is a relational and inessential property of a statement or a belief. Hence the results are different: 'he is sitting', uttered now

[1] Reference to Aristotle's work *Categories* (*Cat.*) is to *Categories*, trans. J. A. Smith, in *The Complete Works of* Aristotle, ed. Jonathan Barnes, 6th printing with corrections, 2 vols. (Princeton: Princeton University Press, 1995).

and later, express two *different* thoughts according to Frege, each with its own eternal truth value; whereas it expresses the *same* belief according to Aristotle, which is true at one time, and false at another. Clearly, then, Aristotle would not accept the claim that different truth values indicate different beliefs. This is opposed to some widely accepted contemporary conceptions. William and Martha Kneale claim that Aristotle made a mistake in claiming this—he should have recognized that the sentences in question express two different propositions (Kneale and Kneale 1962: 54).

We have two clearly different views: according to the Fregean principle, every thought has a determinate truth value, and difference in truth values means a difference in thought. According to the Aristotelian principle, the same statement or belief can be true or false on different occasions; difference in truth value is no indication of difference of belief. In what follows, I shall try to raise doubts about the Fregean principle and offer some support for the Aristotelian principle.

7.5 Same Content—Different Truth Value

The Fregean principle seems convincing in the case of mathematics and logic. Given that the Pythagorean theorem is true, no false sentence could express the same thought as the Pythagorean theorem does. If Frege had these kinds of examples in mind in the first place, it is easy to understand why he adopted the doctrine. But consider a contingent sentence like

(1) The inventor of bifocals was a man.

As it happens, the description picks out Benjamin Franklin, who was indeed a man. So the sentence is true. Now, as far as I know, Frege does not discuss questions arising in connection with alternative possibilities; but such questions are often raised in contemporary philosophy of language or mind. If this statement is contingent, then there is another world where, say, Deborah Franklin invents bifocals, and where the sentence is false. Here we have a phenomenon that, at first sight, is similar to the one we encountered above about the tree and the green leaves, or about someone's sitting or standing: the same sentence can be true in some circumstances (in our world) and false in others (in another possible world), so there is no determinate truth value belonging to this sentence. The view that, in the sequence of sign–sense–reference, each item determines the next is in trouble again. What shall we do?

One option would be to follow the Fregean recipe to the letter, and insist on the determination between sense and reference—between thought and truth value—and claim that (1) *expresses different thoughts in different worlds.* In other words, if we accept without qualifications that thoughts have their truth values essentially, then, given that (1) is true, it is impossible to express the same thought by a false sentence. Hence in a world where Mrs Franklin and not Mr Franklin invented bifocals, the sentence could not express the same thought.

But, contrary to this, it is standard to assume that, in a world where (1) is false, its *content* would nonetheless be the same. A belief expressed by (1) in this world and in another, irrespective of its truth value, would be the same. Philosophers have argued that the content of some of our beliefs depend on contingent features of the world we inhabit, and hence would not be expressible in a world that is appropriately different. Still, I think that even the most committed externalist would allow that at least *some* contents—of a general, descriptive type—do not have their truth value essentially, and hence they can be true in one world and false in another. Denying this would mean that every minute detail of history would change what we mean by our sentences; that every such detail would potentially limit what is thinkable for us. I cannot see any motivation for such a view.

If this is right, then we cannot say that sense (or content) *alone* determines a truth value; we also need the state of the world—what we might call *the circumstances of evaluation*—that is, in this case, the fact that the inventor of bifocals was a man. When we say that sense determines reference, we understand this as *relative to some circumstances of evaluations*. Thus considerations about other possible worlds suggest a departure from the conception that sense alone determines reference, or that thoughts have their truth value essentially. How far this is a departure from Frege I cannot judge, since he is silent on counterfactual situations or other possible worlds. I certainly do not want to suggest that he is committed to the implausible view I sketched above; however, I do think it is possible that he was not entirely aware of further consequences of some of the views he held about this matter.

Returning to the question of the Fregean versus the Aristotelian principle, the case of the inventor of bifocals vindicates the latter. If we ask the question 'Is it always true that a difference in truth value implies difference of thought or belief?', the answer is clearly negative: 'the inventor of bifocals was a man' is true in this world, and false in another, yet its meaning, sense, content, belief, and so on are the same. Is it true that thoughts have their truth values essentially? Evidently not: the same thought in different worlds can have different truth values. Does sense in itself always determine reference? It obviously does not: at least in some cases, sense determines reference only with respect to the state of the world.

7.6 Cross-World and Within-a-World Comparison

If sense determines reference, then sameness of sense implies sameness of reference. However, if sense does not alone determine reference, then we cannot infer from the difference of reference a difference in sense. Recall now Frege's reasoning about the tree and green leaves. He noted the difference in truth value, and inferred a difference in thought. But this move is questionable: for it would be validated only by the unique determination of reference by sense, and this, as we have just seen, is something that cannot generally be upheld. We need a separate argument to show that the principle is applicable to the particular case, and no such argument is provided.

It may be objected that this criticism is not fair. Probably no one will disagree with the claim that the *cross-world* comparison upholds the Aristotelian, rather than the Fregean, principle. It is a further question though what this implies with respect to cases within a world: that is, when, for example, we compare the same sentence uttered at different times. When we said that difference in truth value implies difference in content—continues this objection—we naturally meant this to apply *within a world*. And when we said that sense determines reference, we meant this to apply *relative to a certain state of the world*. But we cannot extend the relativization further. We cannot say that, just as content determines truth value relative to a world, sometimes it determines truth value also relative to further features like a place, a time, or a speaker. The cross-world cases are not analogous to the cross-time, or cross-place, or cross-speaker cases, this objection concludes.

But why should they not be? Take the thoughts that we express by using the classical indexical expressions like 'now' or 'here' or 'you' or 'that'. The characteristic feature of indexical thoughts is that, besides the state of the possible world where they are evaluated, we need further contextual factors to determine their truth value. Now I do not want to suggest that the distinction between circumstances of evaluation and other contextual features should be obliterated; we might need the distinction for various purposes (see Section 7.8 below.) But suppose that someone goes through the following step-by-step reasoning.

We start with mathematical or logical statements. Here it seems plausible that the sameness of thought implies sameness of truth value. Frege says that apprehending a thought and holding it to be true is an event in the inner world of the thinker (Frege 1918: 104). Indeed, it is quite plausible that the thought, whatever we *think*, whatever we *have in mind* when grasping a mathematical statement, the same that is constant on each occasion when we make the statement, is sufficient in itself to determine a truth value.

Recall that determination is understood here as a formal relation, so what is said does not imply that mathematics is somehow mind dependent.

Then we consider contingent statements. We cannot uphold the determination as before; for the same sentence will have different truth values in different worlds. The variation clearly depends on the state of the world, so there is a factor relevant to the determination of truth value that was not present in the previous case. We have two options. First, we could give up the idea that thought *alone* determines reference, and trust the external world to supply the missing determination. Alternatively, we could pack the further determining factor into the thought. The original idea of sense was something that is grasped by the mind, so, to put the matter in a much simplified way, this amounts to choosing whether this further factor should belong to the world or to the contents of our mind. The decision here is almost incontrovertible: the state of the world belongs to the circumstances of evaluation; that is, it does not make a difference to contents. Or, to put it simply, it belongs to the outside world and not to the mind. Thoughts, senses, meanings are constant through many hypothetical variations of the world.

We have arrived at a more complex picture: a sense plus the state of the world result in a definite reference. This should have the consequence that, within a world, there is a definite reference belonging to every sign. But this is not so: even within a world, some sentences change their truth value depending on the context of utterance. For example, the sentence 'You are Judy' is true when addressed to Judy, but false when addressed to her identical twin Trudy. We have a problem with determination again. And I claim that, *just as before, it is up to us* to make a choice about where to locate the source of this. We could build the relevant feature of the context into the sense, as Frege does; in this case, the two sentences would express different thought contents, because the addressees are different. Alternatively, following the hint given by Aristotle, we could insist that sense is autonomous, it is constant throughout utterances, and say that it determines reference not only together with the state of the world, but sometimes also together with some other features supplied by the context—in this case, the person addressed by the utterance.

Suppose that someone had some reasons to opt for this second alternative. One such reason would be to try to preserve the idea—as we saw, certainly present in Frege's work—that thoughts are not only truth evaluable, but also relevant in governing our actions. It can be argued that the cognitive significance of indexical statements is connected to their feature, which is preserved throughout different contexts, and that precisely the same cognitive significance operates in actions. Thus, if we wanted to have a single notion of content, we should try to attribute truth conditions to the very same feature. For me, the main consideration is self-knowledge; again, what falls within the scope of authoritative self-knowledge is the Aristotelian, rather than the Fregean, conception of thought. This can be seen from the fact that there could be Twin situations in different contexts within a world; for example, in facing Judy or facing Trudy, everything may seem the same to the subject, and hence her mental features—including the content of her thoughts—should be the same.

Then we make the same decision as before. We acknowledge the existence of these newly discovered truth-value determining factors, but we place them in the world rather than in the individual mind. Someone could try to justify opting for the other alternative by citing the doctrine that sense determines reference. To this my reply is that we have already given up the idea that sense alone determines reference, without, however, committing ourselves to the view that sense has nothing to do with reference. We just do a bit more of the same. Protesting that this move is not allowed is simply dogmatic. The resulting theory can do justice to the elementary appeal of the doctrine that sense determines reference: since sense alone cannot determine reference anyway, the considerations presented in Section 7.3 support the new theory just as they did the old one. Incidentally, this move would also sort out the somewhat counter-intuitive result we encountered in Section 6.8. If the content of 'You are Judy' is different when facing Judy or Trudy, then one can apparently infallibly response discriminate them. In the view we are considering now, the content of the sentence, and hence the cognitive response to Judy's and Trudy's presence, may be exactly the same—but it will be true evaluated with respect to Judy's being present, and false evaluated with respect to Trudy's being present.

7.7 Non-Indexical Contextualism

A certain resistance to this suggestion may come from the fact that contents are often conceived as propositions, whose truth value, of course, varies from world to world, but not from context to context within a world.

If contents are propositions traditionally conceived, then my proposal is flawed. However, in recent years there has been growing awareness that it is not compulsory to think about contents in this way. This idea has been developed, for example, by Peter Lasersohn (2005) and John MacFarlane (2005, 2007). Indeed, the position I am suggesting here is similar to what MacFarlane calls 'non-indexical contextualism'.

Propositions are evaluated for truth and falsity with respect to certain circumstances of evaluation, and, on the traditional conception of propositions, the circumstances of evaluation include only a possible world. In addition, some authors (e.g., Kaplan 1977: 502 ff.) have argued that times have to be included in the circumstances of evaluation as well. So it is possible that the *same* proposition is expressed at different times, and has different truth values because it is evaluated with respect to different times.

As MacFarlane points out, there is no prima facie theoretical obstacle to including *further factors* among the circumstances of evaluation: for example, standards of precision, or a 'counts-as' parameter (which determines what counts, say, as tall in a certain context). On such a theory, the very same content could be expressed in different contexts, and receive different truth values, if evaluated with respect to different standards of precision, or different parameters of 'counts-as'.

A terminological note: Kaplan originally *contrasted* features of the context and circumstances of evaluation: the former influence the content of an utterance, the latter do not. In MacFarlane's usage, 'context' includes *all* the factors that, in addition to what is invariant in all utterances of the same sentence, determine truth values. These *include* circumstances of evaluation. However, in agreement with Kaplan, he regards circumstances of evaluation as those features of the context that do not influence content. In this terminology, utterances of 'The inventor of bifocals was a man' in this world and another are utterances that take place in different contexts, since the two worlds make different contributions to the truth value of the utterance. In this case, the contextual difference is merely a difference in the circumstances of evaluation, which means that it does not influence the content of the utterances.

Suppose that there are different contexts of who counts as tall—say Holland and Hungary. Someone who holds that 'Chiara is tall' expresses *different content* in these contexts would be an *indexicalist* about 'tall'. However, there is another option: that 'Chiara is tall' expresses the *same content* in these two contexts, but it is to be evaluated with respect to different circumstances of evaluation, which include a 'counts-as' parameter. The claim *that Chiara is tall* is true when evaluated with respect to what counts as tall in Hungary, but false when evaluated with respect to what counts as tall in Holland. This would amount to *non-indexical contextualism* about 'tall' (MacFarlane, 2007).

I would like to suggest a similar theory (though I cannot say whether Lasersohn or MacFarlane would agree with applying the idea in such a broad way). Suppose we are by and large sympathetic to Putnam's theory of natural-kind terms, but would like to adopt a version that is acceptable for the uncompromising internalist position I want to defend. According to this theory, the superficial features of members of natural kinds are held together and explained by some deep-lying mechanisms, and, if someone interacts with a given natural kind in her environment, the *extension* (or *reference*) of her term for that kind is determined by the identity of this deep-lying mechanism. Oscar and Twin Oscar are in natural environments where some superficially similar natural kinds have different inner composition. When they utter the sentence 'There is water in this glass', the content of the sentence is the same. However, the semantics of natural-kind terms is such that, in determining the reference and the truth value of a sentence including a natural-kind term, the *circumstances of evaluation* have to include the actual substance that the subject causally interacts with when assigning a reference to the term. Thus the *same* content, evaluated with respect to Oscar's interactive practices, is about H_2O, while, evaluated with respect to Twin Oscar's interactive practices, is about XYZ.

I do not want to commit myself to this theory; I merely wanted to show that considerations that have been thought to lead to externalism can in fact be accommodated within this framework. The same is true for, say, the semantics of proper names, or indexicals. I can take aboard all sorts of semantic machinery, and agree with a theory about which factors will play a role in the ultimate determination of reference and truth value. The only constraint is that whatever factors are *not* shared by phenomenally identical twin subjects should be conceived, not as making a difference to the content, but rather as being part of the circumstances of evaluation.

Let me try to clarify this move from another angle. As we saw, considerations about contingent statements suggest a departure from the idea that thoughts have their *truth values* essentially. Instead, what is customary to say these days is that thoughts or contents have their *truth conditions* essentially. Here is Robert Stalnaker (1990: 195), for example: 'Everyone agrees that truth-conditions are essential to propositional content as ordinarily conceived: if there are conditions in which your belief will be true and mine false, that is sufficient to establish that our beliefs have different contents.' This is in fact the contemporary version of the Fregean idea that thought is something for which the question of truth arises, or that contents lay a claim of truth upon the world. Now truth values are relatively easy to handle in the sense that there are only two of them, and their difference is clear. But, once we shift from truth values to truth conditions, matters become less obvious: when should we count truth conditions as the same?

Inspired by one of Frege's examples, one might say this: the truth of 'Today is fine', uttered once on 15 March and once on the 16th, depends on the weather's being fine on the 15th in the first case, and on the weather's being fine on the 16th in the second case—thus the truth conditions are obviously different in the two cases. But this is far from obvious. The truth of 'The inventor of bifocals was a man' depends on Mr Franklin's gender in this world, and on Mrs Franklin's gender in another; yet we regard the sentence as having the same truth conditions in both worlds. Why should we not think about the 15th/16th case in an analogous way, maintaining that 'Today is fine' has the same truth conditions in both contexts? These truth conditions must be understood as providing the conditions for the truth of a sentence in a given context. But there does not seem to be anything *inherent* in the notion of truth conditions that would prohibit this—if we allowed world-relative truth conditions, why not allow context-relative truth conditions?

7.8 Double Indexing

The view I am suggesting is this: at least for certain type of context-sensitive expressions, the content of the sentence including this expression is the same throughout different contexts. The context is not constitutive of the content: it contributes to the determination of truth value externally. This does not mean giving up the view that sense determines reference in any plausible sense. The way the context contributes to the truth value of (some) of these sentences is analogous to the way the world contributes to the truth value of contingent sentences. In both cases it is not sense alone, but sense plus some external factors that determine reference.

One crucial element in the proposal is that, when different semantic mechanisms are needed for determining the reference or truth value of expressions and sentences, the 'instructions' for these apparatuses are determined by the *phenomenology* of the content. For example, contents we express by names and descriptions have their characteristic phenomenal features; what it is like to use the same expression as a name or as a description is different. Hence whatever the content of 'The inventor of bifocals is a man' is, it contains instructions, as it were from within, to be evaluated simply with respect to the state of the world. The instructions are not explicit in the consciousness of the subject, but can be recovered by philosophical reasoning and by reflecting on what it is like to use a certain expression. (I describe this in more detail in Farkas forthcoming.) Thus the same content can latch on to different states of the world, resulting in different truth values. The content of other context-sensitive sentences should work in an analogous way: the same content should be able to latch on to different contextual features, again possibly resulting in different truth values.

I shall now discuss some possible objections. David Kaplan argued persuasively that we cannot assimilate the logical role of the circumstances of evaluation to that of the (other) features of the context (see Kaplan 1977: sect. 7; Kaplan 1979: 65–9; remember also that, in Kaplan's terminology, circumstances of evaluation are not part of the context). This mistake is committed by what he calls 'index-theory', which regards *contents* as entailing a function that assigns truth conditions to an *n*-tuple called 'index', consisting of a world, a time, a place, an agent, and possibly other contextual features. This theory faces certain difficulties, which can be resolved, as Kaplan himself suggests, by introducing *double indexing*.

Let me offer an elementary version of double indexing—this is clearly not sufficient for a formal treatment, but it hopefully conveys the basic idea. For present purposes, the relevant features of the context of an utterance are sufficiently determined by *a possible world, an agent, and a time*: the context is given by where and in what situation—in whose company, and so on—that agent is, in that world, at that time. There may be further features of the context; for example, the addressee, or some natural kinds in the environment, and so on, but these are hopefully determined by the above features. This is the *first set* of the features that contributes to the determination of truth value. The *second* is given by the state of affairs with respect to which we want to evaluate the sentence. This could simply be a possible world, or a world at a time. The first set usually determines the references of classical indexical expressions, the second element determines whether what is said of them is true or false. The state of the world relevant to the first set is always the world where the utterance takes place. The world in the second set, with respect to which we evaluate the sentence, may be the same as the first, but it need not be, as, for example, in the case of counterfactual claims. The important thing to keep in mind is that worlds—and possibly other features, like time—should sometimes be counted twice: for example, first as determining a reference for individual expressions, second, as part of the circumstances of evaluation that determine truth values. Hence double indexing.

This theory of double indexing is perfectly compatible with the view I am suggesting, so my view should not be vulnerable to the objections Kaplan makes against the index theory. The logical role of circumstances of evaluation and (other) features of the context is one question, their metaphysical role is another. I agree with separating their logical role—but I claim that, from a metaphysical point of view, there is something common to them: neither of them is constitutive of the content of indexical thoughts. In their separate logical roles, they both contribute to the determination of truth value externally—that is, externally to the contents of our minds.

Kaplan thinks that the index theory is not only technically wrong, but also conceptually misguided. A single semantic feature—something that would yield truth values relative to contexts and circumstances of evaluations—cannot adequately explain the phenomenon of indexicality. Instead, we need first the notion of *character*—this is constant throughout different contexts, and can naturally be thought of as the linguistic meaning of an indexical expression. The task of the character is to assign to the expression, with respect to each context, a second feature, the *content*. The content determines a truth value relative to a world; and consequently, contents have fixed truth values within a world. This view at first sounds obviously incompatible with the theory suggested in this chapter, but, in fact, the incompatibility arises only if we make a further assumption, namely:

> The Psychological Relevance of Contents: contentful mental states (like beliefs) are individuated by their contents, that is, a difference in content implies a difference in the nature of the belief *qua* belief.

I do accept this thesis, and then my proposal does indeed clash with a theory that has contents possessing a single truth value in a world. Whether Kaplan accepts this thesis or not is something I am unable to decide. On the one hand, the earlier quotation in Section 7.3 suggests that he does; on the other hand, some passages like the following suggest that he does not: 'The psychological states, perhaps even the epistemological situations, of Castor and Pollux are alike, yet they assert distinct singular propositions when they each say "My brother was born before me"' (Kaplan 1989: 44). If the singular propositions in question are not psychologically relevant—that is, if they do not contribute to the nature of psychological states—then this chapter is not taking issue with Kaplan's theory. I think I can deal with the technical objection Kaplan raises; deeper conceptual issues would have to be settled by enquiring further into the question of the psychological relevance of contents.

7.9 Relativized Propositions

Another objection is from John Perry's 'The Problem of the Essential Indexical' (Perry 1979). Perry's problem is explicitly about psychological states; and he discusses precisely the view that I am suggesting; that the content of (some) indexical sentences has genuinely context-dependent truth conditions. He introduces the idea of what he calls 'relativized propositions' with considerations similar to the ones presented in this chapter: that once we realize that the same proposition may be true in one world and false in another, this could invite the generalization that the same proposition could be true at one index—time, person, place—and false at another. But Perry thinks that this will not do: a relativized proposition cannot capture the content indexical beliefs.

He reasons as follows. Suppose that I am trying to find the person whose torn sugar bag is leaving a trail on the floor in a supermarket, and then I suddenly realize it is I. When I am trying to find the person who is making a mess, I already believe that someone is making a mess—and therefore I believe that the proposition *that I am making a mess* is true for someone. (I follow Perry in using italics in this way.) But this is not the belief we are after, since it does not have the appropriate connection to actions. The crucial moment is when I realize that the proposition *that I am making a mess* is true for me, and this is something beyond believing the relativized proposition.

What Perry seems to have in mind is this. A belief is a relation between a subject and a proposition, and the proposition is denoted by a that clause. If an indexical sentence expresses a relativized proposition, this is the same throughout all uses of the sentence. So, if I can properly say now that I believe that the proposition *that I am making a mess* is true for someone at some time, then I already have, at this moment, the required belief relation to the relativized proposition expressed by the sentence—and yet I do not believe that I am making a mess (or in any case, the mess involves philosophy and not a torn sugar bag). Therefore a pro-attitude towards a relativized proposition cannot capture the content of an indexical belief.

But this argument cannot be right, and the example about the inventor of bifocals will again help to show why. Consider a reasoning analogous to Perry's. Even before I learnt who invented bifocals, I had thought it could have been a man. So I believed that the proposition *that the inventor of bifocals was a man* was true in some possible world. Since the proposition expressed by the that clause is always the same, I had, already back then, a pro-attitude towards the proposition this sentence expressed. However, this view cannot account for the fact that apparently I have acquired a new belief when I realized that the proposition was true in *this world.* To wit, this was the point when I came to believe that the inventor of bifocals was a man. And this should show, according to the logic of Perry's argument, that believing that the inventor of bifocals was a man is something *beyond* believing the single proposition that is expressed by the sentence throughout different worlds. But this cannot be right—so Perry's original argument cannot be right either.

Part of the problem seems to be that Perry's formulation is ambiguous in an unhelpful way. Here are some things we *can* say: suppose that I have never made a mess in my life and never will, and I am convinced of this; then the proposition that I (K.F.) am making a mess is not true for anyone at any time, and I do not believe it is. However, if Perry's story is true, mess has been made, so there was a time when someone could truly say 'I am making a mess'. I think that Perry's formulation somewhat confusingly combines elements from direct and indirect speech.

Now it is possible that these observations could be a starting point for an argument for the conclusion that first-person beliefs should indeed be analysed according to Perry's suggestion. But, whatever the argument is for this view, it should be based on rather specific observations about the semantics of 'I' in English, and not on the general impossibility of recognizing relativized propositions. And my aim in this chapter is only to show the viability of this option.

7.10 The Inconclusiveness of the Twin Earth Argument

If a theory of relativized propositions is acceptable, this will have important consequences to the debate on externalism and internalism about content.

In 'The Meaning of "Meaning" ', which contains one of the classic arguments for externalism about content, Hilary Putnam (1975a: 219) claims that the following two assumptions are *incompatible*:

I. 'that knowing the meaning of a term is just a matter of being in a certain psychological state' (where the psychological state is understood to be 'narrow', that is, a state which does not presuppose the existence of anything outside the subject.)
II. 'that the meaning of a term (in the sense of "intension") determines its extension (in the sense that sameness of intension entails sameness of extension)'.

The two assumptions being incompatible, one of them has to be given up. The basic intuition in the Twin Earth thought experiment is supposed to be that 'water' refers exclusively to H_2O on Earth, and exclusively to XYZ on Twin Earth. Water, in Putnam's analysis, is whatever bears the same-liquid relation to *this* stuff (pointing to an instance of water), and 'this stuff' picks out H_2O on Earth and XYZ on Twin Earth. Putnam—though he does not argue for this—clearly thinks that, in the case of water, we have to retain assumption (II), and consequently say that 'difference in extension is *ipso facto* a difference in intension' (Putnam 1975a: 234). The rest is all too familiar: an Earthling and his Twin-Earth Doppelgänger are in the same narrow psychological state, 'water' has different extension and ipso facto different meaning for them, hence knowing the meaning of a term cannot be just a matter of being in a narrow psychological state. Retaining (II) has forced us to give up (I).

The argument also extends to concepts, which are the ingredients of the content of mental states: 'water' has a different reference on Earth and Twin Earth; consequently, the WATER concepts on Earth and Twin Earth are different; and hence the contents of the water beliefs of the two planets' inhabitants are different as well.

Arguments like Putnam's proceed by first pointing out that reference or truth value is different for internally identical subjects, and then by arguing further that difference in reference implies a difference in content or meaning. And we can infer from the difference in reference back to the difference in content only if there is a determinate reference belonging to a content. So the assumption that sense (content, meaning, intension, and so on) determines reference is crucial to arguments for externalism.

Moreover, what these arguments need is a specific understanding of this assumption. We saw in the earlier discussion that no plausible version of the sense-determines-reference doctrine can claim that sense always *alone* determines reference. All upholders of the doctrine have to agree that—at least in the case of some contingent statements—sense, plus something *beyond* (that is, not constitutive of) sense determines reference. According to the usual understanding, this outside factor is exhausted by the state of the world. However, I have argued that there is nothing inherent to the notion of content, truth condition, or reference determination that would prohibit us counting some further features—notably, certain features of the context—among these outside factors.

But, if this is a viable option, then the externalist argument is not conclusive. For we could accept the basic intuition of the Twin-Earth argument—that 'water' refers to different things on Earth and Twin Earth—*and* accept the doctrine that sense (plus some outside factors) determines reference, and still hold that the sense of 'water' is the same on the two planets. All we would have to do is to count certain features of the environment—like the chemical structure of stuff we causally interact with—among the outside (that is, not sense-constituting) factors that contribute to the determination of reference.

7.11 Internalism with Truth Conditionality

Summing up. According to a widely accepted view, beliefs are individuated by their contents, in the sense that difference in content implies difference in beliefs. Moreover, contents should be conceived as propositions, and a proposition has a unique truth value in a world. As a consequence, beliefs with different truth values are themselves different. In this chapter, I have tried to challenge this view: developing an idea found in Aristotle, I have maintained that it is possible to conceive the content of some beliefs—content that is psychologically relevant—as changing its truth value within the same world, depending on further features of the context. I have argued that this does not force us to give up the doctrine that sense determines reference; it is only that we have to acknowledge that sense plus some other factors determine reference, and this acknowledgement has been done anyway.

Considerations like the ones I elaborated in the previous chapters about self-knowledge may incline one towards internalism about content. However, a constant worry about internalism has been that, as the Twin-Earth arguments allegedly show, it would force us to give up the claim that content is truth conditional (or reference determining). And, if content is not truth conditional, then it becomes unintelligible how what we say makes a claim about the world. We aim at the truth with our statements; but, if these statements are not truth evaluable, the whole enterprise is thwarted.

I believe the considerations advanced above should dispel the worries about truth conditionality. Since we recognize that truth conditions are not always absolute, but they have to operate within a world, there is no obstacle to the view that states that, similarly, sometimes they operate within further features of the context. If a statement lays a claim of truth about the world, it is still up to the world to determine whether it is actually true or not. Similarly, some claims of truth are laid in a context, and the other features of the context must determine their validity. There is no need for the internalist to give up the idea that contents are truth conditional.

This concludes the project of this book. I have defended a certain conception of the mental, one I regard as developing Descartes's fundamental insight about the mind: that the mind is essentially revealed from the subject's point of view. I have shown that this conception lies at the heart of contemporary internalist theories. I have considered an objection against the notion of internally individuated content and found it wanting. Hopefully, we can now give back the subject and her point of view the proper place they deserve.

References

When a title has been reprinted, page references refer to the reprint.

Aristotle (1995 edn.). *The Complete Works of* Aristotle, ed. Jonathan Barnes, 6th printing with corrections, 2 vols. (Princeton: Princeton University Press).

Armstrong, D. M. (1968). *A Materialist Theory of the Mind* (London: Routledge and Kegan Paul).

Blackburn, Simon (1984). *Spreading the Word* (Oxford: Clarendon Press).

Block, Ned (1996). 'Mental Paint and Mental Latex'. *Philosophical Issues*, 7: 19–49.

Block, Ned, and Stalnaker, Robert (1999). 'Conceptual Analysis, Dualism, and the Explanatory Gap'. *Philosophical Review*, 108: 1–46.

Bloom, Paul (2004). *Descartes' Baby: How the Science of Child Development Explains what Makes us Human* (New York: Basic Books).

Boghossian, Paul A. (1989). 'Content and Self-Knowledge'. *Philosophical Topics*, 17: 5–26.

Boghossian, Paul A. (1994). 'The Transparency of Mental Content'. *Philosophical Perspectives*, 8: 33–50.

Boghossian, Paul A. (1996). 'Analyticity Reconsidered'. *Noûs*, 30: 360–91.

Boghossian, Paul A. (1997). 'What the Externalist Can Know A Priori'. *Proceedings of the Aristotelian Society*, 97: 161–75.

Bonjour, Lawrence (1998). *In Defense of Pure Reason: A Rationalist Account of a Priori Justification* (Cambridge: Cambridge University Press).

Brown, Jessica (2004). *Anti-individualism and Knowledge* (Cambridge, MA: MIT Press).

Brueckner, Anthony (1990). 'Scepticism about Knowledge of Content'. *Mind*, 99: 447–52.

Burge, Tyler (1979). 'Individualism and the Mental', in Peter A. French, Theodore E. Uehling, Jr., and K. Howard (eds.), *Midwest Studies in Philosophy IV* (Minneapolis: University of Minnesota Press), 73–121.

Burge, Tyler (1986). 'Cartesian Error and the Objectivity of Perception', in Pettit and McDowell 1986: 117–36.

Burge, Tyler (1988). 'Individualism and Self-Knowledge'. *Journal of Philosophy*, 85: 649–63.

Burge, Tyler (1996). 'Our Entitlement to Self-Knowledge'. *Proceedings of the Aristotelian Society*, 96: 91–116.

Byrne, Alex, and Tye, Michael (2006). 'Qualia ain't in the Head'. *Noûs*, 40: 241–55.

Chalmers, David (2002). 'The Components of Content', in David Chalmers (ed.), *Philosophy of Mind: Classical and Contemporary Readings* (Oxford: Oxford University Press), 608–33.

Clark, Austen (1993). *Sensory Qualities* (Oxford: Oxford University Press).

Cottingham, John (1978). ' "A Brute to the Brutes?": Descartes' Treatment of Animals'. *Philosophy*, 53: 551–9.

Cottingham, John (1992). 'Cartesian Dualism: Theology, Metaphysics and Science', in John Cottingham (ed.), *The Cambridge Companion to Descartes* (Cambridge: Cambridge University Press), 236–57.

Crane, Tim (1991). 'All the Difference in the World'. *Philosophical Quarterly*, 41: 1–25.

Crane, Tim (1995). 'The Mental Causation Debate'. *Proceedings of the Aristotelian Society*, supplementary volume, 211–36.

Crane, Tim (2001). *Elements of Mind* (Oxford: Oxford University Press).

Davidson, Donald (1987). 'Knowing One's Own Mind'. *Proceedings and Addresses of the American Philosophical Association*, 60: 441–58; repr. in Quassim Cassam (ed.), *Self-Knowledge* (Oxford: Oxford University Press, 1994), 43–64.

Davies, Martin (1998). 'Externalism, Architecturalism and Epistemic Warrant', in Wright et al. 1998: 321–61.

Dennett, Daniel C. (1976). 'Conditions of Personhood', in Amelie Oksenberg Rorty (ed.), *The Identities of Persons* (Berkeley and Los Angeles: University of California Press), 175–96.

Dennett, Daniel C. (1988). 'Quining Qualia', in A. Marcel and E. Bisiach (eds.), *Consciousness in Modern Science* (Oxford: Oxford University Press); repr. at <http://cogprints.org/254/00/quinqual.htm>.

Descartes, René (1996 edn.). *Œuvres de Descartes*, ed. Charles Adam and Paul Tannery. 11 vols. (Paris: Vrin/CNRS 1966–76).

Descartes, René (1984–5 edn.). *The Philosophical Writings of Descartes*, vols. i and ii, ed. and trans. John Cottingham, Robert Stoothoff, and Dugald Murdoch (Cambridge: Cambridge University Press).

Descartes, René (1991 edn.). *The Philosophical Writings of Descartes*, vol. iii (a selection of Descartes's letters), ed. and trans. John Cottingham, Robert Stoothoff, Dugald Murdoch, and Anthony Kenny (Cambridge: Cambridge University Press).

Devitt, Michael, and Sterelny, Kim (1987). *Language and Reality* (Cambridge, MA: MIT Press).

Dretske, Fred (1969). *Seeing and Knowing* (Chicago: University of Chicago Press).

Dretske, Fred (1995). *Naturalizing the Mind* (Cambridge, MA: MIT Press).

Dummett, Michael (1970). 'Wang's Paradox'; repr. in Dummett, *Truth and Other Enigmas* (London: Duckworth, 1978), 248–68.

Dummett, Michael (1975). 'Frege's Distinction between Sense and Reference'; repr. in Dummett, *Truth and Other Enigmas* (London: Duckworth, 1978), 116–144.

Ebbs, Gary (2005). 'Why Scepticism about Self-Knowledge is Self-Undermining'. *Analysis*, 65: 237–44.

Evans, Gareth (1982). *The Varieties of Reference* (Oxford: Clarendon Press).

Evans, Gareth (1985). 'Understanding Demonstratives'; repr. in Paul Yourgrau (ed.), *Demonstratives* (Oxford: Oxford University Press, 1990), 71–96.

Everett, Anthony (1996). 'Qualia and Vagueness'. *Synthese*, 106: 205–26.

Falvey, Kevin, and Owens, Joseph (1994). 'Externalism, Self-Knowledge, and Skepticism'. *Philosophical Review*, 103: 107–37.

Farkas, Katalin (2003). 'What is Externalism?' *Philosophical Studies*, 112: 187–208.

Farkas, Katalin (2005). 'The Unity of Descartes's Thought'. *History of Philosophy Quarterly*, 22: 17–30.

Farkas, Katalin (2006). 'Indiscriminability and the Sameness of Appearance'. *Proceedings of the Aristotelian Society*, 106: 205–25.

Farkas, Katalin (forthcoming). 'Phenomenal Intentionality without Compromise'. *Monist*, 91.

Fodor, Jerry (1987). *Psychosemantic* (Cambridge, MA: MIT Press).

Fodor, Jerry (1990). *A Theory of Content and Other Essays* (Cambridge, MA: MIT Press).

Fodor, Jerry (1994). *The Elm and the Expert* (Cambridge, MA: MIT Press).

Frankfurt, Harry (1971). 'Freedom of the Will and the Concept of a Person'. *Journal of Philosophy*, 68: 5–20.

Frege, Gottlob (1892). 'On Sense and Reference'; repr. in A. W. Moore (ed.), *Meaning and Reference* (Oxford: Oxford University Press, 1993), 23–42.

Frege, Gottlob (1918). 'The Thought'; repr. in Simon Blackburn and Keith Simmons (eds.), *Truth* (Oxford: Oxford University Press, 1999), 85–104.

Freud, Sigmund (1915). 'The Unconscious'; repr. in Freud, *On Metapsychology*, trans. from the German under the general editorship of James Strachey, ed. Angela Richards (Harmondsworth, Penguin Books, 1991), 159–222.

Goldberg, Sanford C. (2000). 'Externalism and Authoritative Knowledge of Content: A New Incompatibilist Strategy'. *Philosophical Studies*, 100: 51–79.

Goldman, Alvin (1976). 'Discrimination and Perceptual Knowledge'. *Journal of Philosophy*, 73: 771–91.

Goodman, Nelson (1951). *The Structure of Appearance* (Cambridge, MA: Harvard University Press).

Graff, Delia (2001). 'Phenomenal Continua and the Sorites'. *Mind*, 110: 905–35.

Grahek, Nikola (2001). *Feeling Pain and Being in Pain* (Oldenburg: Bibliotheks- und Informationssystem der Universitaet Oldenburg).

Gulick, Robert van (2004). 'Consciousness', in Edward N. Zalta (ed.), *The Stanford Encyclopedia of Philosophy (Fall 2004 Edition)*, <http://plato.stanford.edu/archives/fall2004/entries/consciousness/>.

Guttenplan, Samuel (1994) (ed.), *A Companion to the Philosophy of Mind* (Oxford: Basil Blackwell).

Harman, Gilbert (1973). *Thought* (Princeton: Princeton University Press).

Heil, John (1988). 'Privileged Access'. *Mind*, 47: 238–51.

Heil, John (1998). *Philosophy of Mind: A Contemporary Introduction* (London: Routledge).

Horgan, Terence, and Tienson, John (2002). 'The Intentionality of Phenomenology and the Phenomenology of Intentionality', in David Chalmers (ed.), *Philosophy of Mind: Classical and Contemporary Readings* (Oxford: Oxford University Press), 520–31.

Horgan, Terence, Tienson, John, and Graham, George (2004). 'Phenomenal Intentionality and the Brain in a Vat', in Richard Schantz (ed.), *The Externalist Challenge: New Studies on Cognition and Intentionality* (Berlin: Walter de Gruyter), 297–317.

Hume, David (1739–40). *Treatise of Human Nature*. 2nd edn., ed. L. A. Selby-Bigge, rev. P. H. Nidditch (Oxford: Clarendon Press, 1978).

Jackson, Frank, and Pettit, Philip (1988). 'Functionalism and Broad Content'; repr. in Pessin and Goldberg 1996: 219–30.

Jackson, Frank, and Pinkerton, R. J. (1973). 'On an Argument against Sensory Items'. *Mind*, 82: 269–72.

Kahn, Charles H. (1992). 'Aristotle on Thinking', in Martha Nussbaum and Amelia Oksenberg Rorty (eds.), *Essays on Aristotle's* De Anima (Oxford: Oxford University Press), 109–27.

Kaplan, David (1977). 'Demonstratives'; repr. in Joseph Almog, John Perry, and Howard Wettstein (eds.), *Themes from Kaplan* (Oxford: Oxford University Press, 1989), 481–563.

Kaplan, David (1979). 'On the Logic of Demonstratives'; repr. in Nathan Salmon and Scott Soames (eds.), *Propositions and Attitudes* (Oxford: Oxford University Press, 1988), 66–82.

Kaplan, David (1989). 'Thoughts on Demonstratives'; repr. in P. Yourgrau (ed.), *Demonstratives* (Oxford: Oxford University Press, 1990), 34–49.

Kenny, Anthony (1989). *The Metaphysics of Mind* (Oxford: Oxford University Press).

Kim, Jaegwon (1996). *Philosophy of Mind* (Boulder, CO: Westview).

Kneale, William, and Kneale, Martha (1962). *The Development of Logic* (Oxford: Oxford University Press).

Kripke, Saul A. (1972). *Naming and Necessity*; repr. as a book (Oxford: Blackwell, 1980).

La Mettrie, Julien Offray de (1748). *L'Homme machine* (Leyden: Elie Luzac).

Lasersohn, Peter (2005). 'Context Dependence, Disagreement, and Predicates of Personal Taste'. *Linguistics and Philosophy*, 28: 643–86.

Lear, Jonathan (1988). *Aristotle: The Desire to Understand* (Cambridge: Cambridge University Press).

Lewis, David (1966). 'An Argument for the Identity Theory'. *Journal of Philosophy*, 63: 17–25.

Loar, Brian (1988). 'Social Content and Psychological Content', in Robert Grimm and Daniel Merrill (eds.), *Contents of Thought* (Tucson: University of Arizona Press), 99–110.

Loar, Brian (2003). 'Phenomenal Intentionality as the Basis of Mental Content', in Martin Hahn and Bjørn Ramberg (eds.), *Reflections and Replies: Essays on the Philosophy of Tyler Burge* (Cambridge, MA: MIT Press), 229–58.

Locke, John (1690). *Essay Concerning Human Understanding*, ed. P. H. Nidditch (Oxford: Oxford University Press, 1975).

Loewer, Barry, and Rey, Georges (1991) (eds.), *Meaning in Mind: Fodor and his Critics* (Oxford and Cambridge, MA: Blackwell).

Lowe, E. J. (1996). *Subjects of Experience* (Cambridge: Cambridge University Press).

Ludlow, Peter, and Martin, Norah (1998) (eds.), *Externalism and Self-Knowledge* (Stanford, CA: CSLI Publications).

McCulloch, Gregory (1995). *The Mind and its World* (London and New York: Routledge).

MacDonald, Cynthia (1998). 'Externalism and Authoritative Self-Knowledge', in Wright et al. 1998: 124–54.

McDowell, John (1982). 'Criteria, Defeasibility and Knowledge'; repr. in Jonathan Dancy (ed.), *Perceptual Knowledge* (Oxford: Oxford University Press, 1988), 209–19 .

McDowell, John (1986). 'Singular Thought and the Extent of Inner Space', in Pettit and McDowell 1986: 136–168.

McDowell, John (1992). 'Putnam on Mind and Meaning'. *Philosophical Topics*, 20(1): 35–48; repr. in Pessin and Goldberg 1996: 305–17.

McDowell, John (1994). *Mind and World* (Cambridge, MA: Harvard University Press).

MacFarlane, John (2005). 'Making Sense of Relative Truth'. *Proceedings of the Aristotelian Society*, 105: 321–39.

MacFarlane, John (2007). 'Semantic Minimalism and Nonindexical Contextualism', in Gerhard Preyer and Georg Peter (eds.), *Context-Sensitivity and Semantic Minimalism: Essays on Semantics and Pragmatics.* (Oxford: Oxford University Press), 240–50.

McGinn, Colin (1982). 'The Structure of Content', in Andrew Woodfield (ed.), *Thought and Object* (Oxford: Clarendon Press), 207–58.

McKinsey, Michael (1991). 'Anti-Individualism and Privileged Access'. *Analysis*, 51: 9–16.

McLaughlin, Brian P., and Tye, Michael (1998). 'Is Content-Externalism Compatible with Privileged Access?' *Philosophical Review*, 107: 349–80.

Manson, Neil Campbell (2000). ' "A Tumbling Ground for Whimsies"? The History and Contemporary Role of the Conscious/Unconscious Contrast', in Tim Crane and Sarah Patterson (eds.), *The History of the Mind–Body Problem* (London: Routledge), 148–68.

Martin, M. G. F. (2004). 'The Limits of Self-Awareness'. *Philosophical Studies*, 120: 37–89.

Martin, M. G. F. (2005). 'On Being Alienated', in Tamar Szabo Gendler and John Hawthorne (eds.), *Perceptual Experience* (Oxford: Oxford University Press), 354–409.

Matthews, Gareth B. (1977). 'Consciousness and Life'. *Philosophy*, 52: 13–26; repr. in David Rosenthal (ed.), *The Nature of Mind* (Oxford: Oxford University Press, 1991), 63–70.

Mills, Eugene (2002). 'Fallibility and the Phenomenal Sorites'. *Noûs*, 36: 384–407.

Nagel, Thomas (1974). 'What is it Like to be a Bat?' *Philosophical Review*, 83: 435–50.

Nagel, Thomas (1986). *The View from Nowhere* (New York and Oxford: Oxford University Press).

Newman, Anthony (2005). 'Two Grades of Internalism (Pass and Fail)'. *Philosophical Studies*, 122: 153–69.

Nuccetelli, Susana (1999). 'What Anti-Individualists Cannot Know A Priori'. *Analysis*, 59: 48–51.

Nuccetelli, Susana (2003) (ed.), *New Essays on Semantic Externalism and Self-Knowledge* (Cambridge, MA: MIT Press).

Nussbaum, Martha, and Putnam, Hilary (1992). 'Changing Aristotle's Mind', in Nussbaum and Rorty 1992: 27–56.

Nussbaum, Martha, and Rorty, Amelia Oksenberg (1992) (eds.), *Essays on Aristotle's* De Anima (Oxford: Oxford University Press).

Owens, Joseph (2003). 'Anti-Individualism, Indexicality and Character', in Martin Hahn and Bjørn Ramberg (eds.), *Reflections and Replies: Essays on the Philosophy of Tyler Burge* (Cambridge, MA: MIT Press), 77–100.

Parfit, Derek (1984). *Reasons and Persons* (Oxford: Oxford University Press).

Perry, John (1977). 'Frege on Demonstratives'; repr. in P. Yourgrau (ed.), *Demonstratives* (Oxford: Oxford University Press, 1990), 50–70.

Perry, John (1979). 'The Problem of the Essential Indexical'; repr. in Nathan Salmon and Scott Soames (eds.), *Propositions and Attitudes* (Oxford: Oxford University Press, 1988), 83–101.

Pessin, Andrew and Goldberg, Sanford (1996) (eds.) *The Twin Earth Chronicles* (Armonk, NY, and London: M. S. Sharpe).

Pettit, Philip (1986). 'Broad-Minded Explanation and Psychology', in Pettit and McDowell 1986: 17–58.

Pettit, Philip, and McDowell, John (1986) (eds.), *Subject, Thought and Context* (Oxford: Clarendon Press).

Pitt, David (2004). 'The Phenomenology of Cognition or What is it Like to Think that P?' *Philosophy and Phenomenological Research*, 69: 1–36.

Putnam, Hilary (1967). 'The Nature of Mental States'; repr. in Putnam 1975b: 429–40.

Putnam, Hilary (1970). 'Is Semantics Possible?'; repr. in Putnam 1975b: 139–52.

Putnam, Hilary (1975a). 'The Meaning of "Meaning" '; repr. in Putnam 1975b: 215–27.

Putnam, Hilary (1975b). *Mind, Language and Reality* (Cambridge: Cambridge University Press).

Putnam, Hilary (1981). *Reason, Truth and History* (Cambridge: Cambridge University Press).

Putnam, Hilary (1999). *The Threefold Cord: Mind, Body and World* (New York: Columbia University Press).

Raffman, Diana (2001). 'Is Perceptual Indiscriminability Nontransitive?' *Philosophical Topics*, 28: 153–75.

Robinson, Howard (1972). 'Professor Armstrong on "Non-Physical Sensory Items" '. *Mind*, 81: 84–6.

Robinson, Howard (1994). *Perception* (London and New York: Routledge).

Rorty, Amelie Oksenberg (1988). 'Persons and Personae', in Rorty, *Mind in Action: Essays in the Philosophy of Mind* (Boston: Beacon Press), 27–46.

Rorty, Richard (1970). 'Incorrigibility as the Mark of the Mental'. *Journal of Philosophy*, 67: 329–424.

Rorty, Richard (1980). *Philosophy and the Mirror of Nature* (Princeton: Princeton University Press).
Russell, Bertrand (1910–11). 'Knowledge by Aquaintance and Knowledge by Description'. *Proceedings of the Aristotelian Society*, 11: 108–28; repr. in Russell, *Mysticism and Logic* (London: Allen & Unwin, 1963), 152–67.
Ryle, Gilbert (1948). *The Concept of Mind* (London: Hutchinson).
Salmon, Nathan (1986). *Frege's Puzzle* (Cambridge, MA: MIT Press).
Searle, John R. (1983). *Intentionality* (Cambridge: Cambridge University Press).
Segal, Gabriel (1989). 'Seeing What is not There'. *Philosophical Review*, 98: 189–214.
Segal, Gabriel (2000). *A Slim Book about Narrow Content* (Cambridge, MA: MIT Press).
Sellars, Wilfrid (1956). *Empiricism and the Philosophy of Mind*; republished as a book (Cambridge, MA: Harvard University Press, 1997).
Shields, Christopher (2005). 'Aristotle's Psychology', in Edward N. Zalta (ed.), *The Stanford Encyclopedia of Philosophy (Summer 2005 Edition)*, <http://plato.stanford.edu/archives/sum2005/entries/aristotle-psychology/>.
Siegel, Susanna (2004). 'Indiscriminability and the Phenomenal'. *Philosophical Studies*, 120: 90–112.
Siewert, Charles P. (1998). *The Significance of Consciousness* (Princeton: Princeton University Press).
Snowdon, Paul (1990). 'Persons, Animals, and Ourselves'; repr. in Tim Crane and Katalin Farkas (eds.), *Metaphysics: A Guide and Anthology* (Oxford: Oxford University Press, 2004), 580–98.
Sorensen, Roy (1998). 'Logical Luck'. *Philosophical Quarterly*, 48: 319–34.
Sousa, Ronald de (2002). 'Twelve Varieties of Subjectivity: Dividing in Hopes of Conquest', in J. M. Larrazabal and L. A. Pérez Miranda (eds.), *Knowledge, Language, and Representation* (Dordrecht: Kluwer), 135–51.
Stalnaker, Robert (1990). 'Narrow Content'; repr. in Stalnaker, *Context and Content* (Oxford: Clarendon Press, 1999), 195–210.
Stalnaker, Robert (2001). 'On Considering a Possible World as Actual'. *Proceedings of the Aristotelian Society*, supplementary volume, 141–56.
Strawson, Galen (1994). *Mental Reality* (Cambridge, MA: MIT Press).
Strawson, Peter F. (1959). *Individuals*; repr. (London and New York: Routledge, 1993).

Sturgeon, Scott (2000). *Matters of Mind* (London and New York: Routledge).

Tolstoy, Leo (1873–7). *Anna Karenina*, trans. Constance Garnett. Bartleby.com internet edition, <http://www.bartleby.com/316/>.

Travis, Charles (1985). 'Vagueness, Observation and Sorites'. *Mind*, 94: 345–66.

Tye, Michael (1995). *Ten Problems of Consciousness* (Cambridge, MA: MIT Press).

Tye, Michael (2002). 'Representationalism and the Transparency of Experience'. *Noûs*, 36: 137–51.

Weatherson, Brian (2007). 'Intrinsic vs. Extrinsic Properties', in Edward N. Zalta (ed.), *The Stanford Encyclopedia of Philosophy (Spring 2007 Edition)*, <http://plato.stanford.edu/archives/spr2007/entries/intrinsic-extrinsic/>.

Wiggins, David (2001). *Sameness and Substance Renewed* (Cambridge: Cambridge University Press).

Wilkes, Kathleen (1992). '*Psuché* versus the Mind', in Nussbaum and Rorty 1992: 109–27.

Williamson, Timothy (1990). *Identity and Discrimination* (Oxford: Basil Blackwell).

Williamson, Timothy (1995). 'Is Knowing a State of Mind?' *Mind*, 104: 533–65.

Williamson, Timothy (2000). *Knowledge and its Limits* (Oxford: Oxford University Press).

Wright, Crispin, Smith, Barry C., and MacDonald, Cynthia (1998) (eds.), *Knowing our own Minds* (Oxford: Oxford University Press).

Index

Lightning Source UK Ltd.
Milton Keynes UK
18 January 2011

165848UK00001B/7/P

9 780199 230327